# a is for apple

Alan Saunders is a writer and broadcaster with a special interest in food, film and philosophy. He joined the Science Unit of ABC Radio National in 1987 and started *The Food Program* in 1988. Since 1997 he has presented *The Comfort Zone*, an acclaimed weekly review of architecture and design, food and gardens. In 1992, Alan was awarded the prestigious Pascall Prize for critical writing and broadcasting.

To Robyn Williams
in gratitude and affection.

# A

## is for apple

## Alan Saunders

𝒱

VINTAGE

A Vintage book
Published by
Random House Australia Pty Ltd
20 Alfred Street, Milsons Point, NSW 2061
http://www.randomhouse.com.au

Sydney   New York   Toronto
London   Auckland   Johannesburg

First edition published by William Heinemann 1995
This edition published 1999

National Library of Australia
Cataloguing-in-Publication Data
Saunders, Alan, 1954–
A is for apple.

ISBN 0 091 84062 7

1. Food. 2. Gastronomy. I. Title

641.013

Design by Yolande Gray
Typeset by Midland Typesetters, Maryborough, Victoria.
Printed and bound by Griffin Press Pty Ltd, Netley, South Australia

10 9 8 7 6 5 4 3 2 1

**contents**

# introduction

This book will do little to further serious scholarship on the subject of food; it has no case to argue, no thesis to defend, and it flutters from idea to idea in a way that most of us hoped had long since been abandoned by grown-up food writers. My excuse for the form, though not for the content, of my book is that I took it from one of the very best of my predecessors, the late M.F.K. Fisher, whose *Alphabet for Gourmets* was published in 1949. The differences between us are the differences between a truly serious writer and the merely earnest one who comes plodding after her.

Though this is in no sense a collection of articles previously published, I have, Frankenstein-like, put together parts of it from the limbs, vital organs and dismembered torsos of earlier writings. I owe a considerable debt of gratitude to all those who commissioned these writings and made me think thoughts I wouldn't otherwise have thought: Jane Adams of *Mentelle Notes*, Deborah Bogle of the *Australian*, Peter Browne of *Modern Times*, Bernard Cohen of *Editions*, Brian Courtis and Michelle Fincke of *Australian Way*, William Fraser of the *Sydney Morning Herald*, Helen Greenwood of *Plenty* and the *Sydney Morning Herald*, Jenny Lee of *Meanjin*, Cassandra Pybus and the 1993 Salamanca Place Writers' Festival, the organising committees of the Sixth Symposium of Australian Gastronomy and of the 1992 Melbourne Writers' Festival.

Daryl Colqhoun suggested to me that Q might stand for Qualia and David Dale was gracious enough to sanction my theft from him of the idea that X might stand for Xanadu.

There would have been no book at all were it not for Richard Deutch, my agent, and Sue Hines of Reed Books. Christine Cremen read some early drafts and sat patiently on the end of the phone while I read to her. I am ever thankful for her patience and encouragement.

Finally, I am grateful to my good friend and colleague Cherry Ripe, the breadth of whose knowledge is matched only by the generosity with which she shares it.

For the paperback edition my thanks go to Hazel Flynn of Random House for putting me between soft covers. I have made a number of small amendments to the text with a view to shortening, tightening, improving or simply rendering grammatical that which (unaccountably) had seemed all right the first time round.

# a is for apple

'What's that?' asked the woman.

'You don't want to know,' replied the man. He held it out to her on the end of a pointed stick. In some parts it was pink, in others red. It glistened in the morning sun, she noticed, and a faint vapour seemed to be rising from it. The smell was disgusting, and it was the smell that she noticed most of all. Indeed, ever since the Old Man evicted them, her nose had been a perpetual riot of bad smells: the close, wet aroma of the leaves that just now seemed to be falling all the time from the trees; the strange, disgusting animals with four legs and the brown stuff they left all over the place; the brown stuff that she, to her intense humiliation, now found that she had to leave all over the place; even her own body, even his. Especially his.

Below them, on the infinite lowlands, forests, thick

with life, resounding with the noise of the beasts to which they were home, stretched away towards the zone where the sun had just risen. Clean rivers coiled in and out of the trees. Across the plains herds of swift animals ran for the sheer pleasure of running, heedless of predators (for those creatures which had been made predators had as yet to understand the nature of their office). It was the dawn of all things, the breakfast of creation.

'Eat a bit,' said the man. 'I've tried some, it's all right,' he added when he saw the look of disgust pass across her face.

'Is it one of the things we're allowed to eat?' she asked.

'I'm not sure those rules apply any more.'

'The Old Man was very specific.'

'What more can He do to us than He's done already?'

She yielded and ate. It was every bit as disgusting as she'd feared it would be; warm and slimy, it caught in her throat and she almost gagged, but she managed to get it down.

She hated this sort of thing. Whatever the subject— food, shelter or that new sticky thing that they'd started to do together—she always seemed now to be giving in to him, and it looked as though this state of affairs would continue for some time. All he had to do to win an argument was to remind her of their situation and imply that she was the one who had brought them to it. At first she had argued with him, but now she was beginning to believe it herself, even though she could still summon up recollection of the contempt she had felt when he'd blabbed to the Old Man. Of course, the Old Man knew everything (as He never tired of pointing out to them), so there had been no real question of concealing from Him the fact that they'd eaten that bloody fruit. But, really, the sight of the man standing there in one of those ludicrous little aprons they'd quickly run up out of fig leaves when they realised that they were naked, standing there trembling in the cool of the evening and sobbing 'She made me do it,' had severely dampened the respect she'd allowed him for having been first on the scene and for having given names to every beast of the field and every fowl of the air.

But day by day the strength of her contempt seemed to fade, as though shrivelling in the harsh sunlight of the world outside the garden. There were even moments when what she had at first thought of as his most ludicrous char-acteristics—the bombast, the pathetic insistence that he was protecting her from a new and hostile world—began to seem almost charming. This was such a moment.

'You were very brave to eat it,' she said. 'Where does it come from?'

'From one of those animals,' he said. 'What's it called now?'

'Why ask me? You're the one who gave names to every beast of the field and every fowl of the air. Do you mean one of those big ones? A deer, perhaps?'

'Yes, that's it, a deer. Well, I was watching it walk

through the forest and it seemed to be walking very slowly. Then it sort of leant against a tree and slid to the ground. I came up closer and it was . . . It was dead.'

This was not a word they used very often, since the discovery of it, which had occurred as soon as they ate the fruit, had been such a shock to them both. It was bigger than the discovery that not having any clothes on meant you were naked, and worse, really, because it seemed to represent a reality which no fig leaf could conceal.

The woman ignored the implication of what he had told her and took another piece from the end of the stick. She was beginning to enjoy it.

'So this used to belong to the deer?' she asked, intrigued but not really puzzled (for the concept of private property was as yet only rudimentary, and it had not occurred to them to restrict rights of ownership to themselves).

'No,' he said. 'You don't understand. This *is* the deer.'

'What!' She spat dead deer. 'That's disgusting!'

'Well, it would only have stayed there getting smelly— and, anyway, the Old Man did give us dominion over the fish of the sea, and over the fowl of the air, and over every living thing that moveth upon the earth.'

'Yes,' she said, wiping the horrible dead-deer grease from her lips, 'and He also told us what to eat. Don't you remember? Every herb-bearing seed that is upon the face of all the earth, and every tree, in which is the fruit of a tree yielding seed.'

'Well, the Old Man isn't here any more, and I thought this would make a change from apples. You're always saying how you can't face another apple.'

This was true: their relationship with the fruit did now have its ambiguities. On the first evening—after the Old Man's archangelic bouncer had shown them the door—they'd taken shelter under an apple tree. The following morning they ate the fruit that had fallen about them during the night. It was their first breakfast outside the garden and their first intimation that this could be a tense meal, a time of wordless glances and unspoken recriminations. They had eaten many apples since then—small, bitter, crabby things they were too—but never without a sense of something forever lost that soured their love for each other.

But, of course, it hadn't as yet really been a meal. Now, though, as he sat down beside her, the horrible piece of deer wobbling on its stick, and she began to take an uneasy pleasure in its dead flavour, they both knew that something had changed.

'I've been thinking,' she said. 'These deer, do they die often?'

'Only once,' he replied. It was the world's first joke. This would have been an impossibility in the days when the Old Man ran their lives and everything was perfect, including the fit between meaning and word, word and apprehension; but the woman stared coldly at him and he died the first comic's death.

'What I mean,' she continued, ignoring the major contribution he had just falteringly made to human understanding, 'is that if we can't find many that are already dead, we could sort of ...'

'Help them?'

'Yes, that's it, help them.'

In the beginning they helped them by throwing stones at them as they ran between the trees. Then they learned that a stone will go further and find its mark more surely if propelled with the assistance of a loop of soft animal skin. Next, they tried pointed wooden sticks, at first thrown with the hand and later with the help of a piece of twine tied to each end of another stick and pulled back as far as the stick would bend. It was around this time— as their weapons grew more accurate and more deadly, and they were able to stand farther and farther from their quarry—that he declared the whole business too dangerous for her. Better that she stay behind and learn the mysteries of making the dead animals good to eat. At first, she didn't mind this, because she knew what he knew but was reluctant to admit: that the hot, evanescent yellow thing they used to make the dead flesh warm and tender was itself a wild creature which it took much skill to tame. Only when she had thoroughly learned its mysteries did he announce to her that they weren't really mysteries after all and that the way of the hunter and the deer in the forest was the true mystery.

So great, indeed, was this new mystery that sometimes

he was away for all the hours of daylight, pursuing his prey through the forest or across the plain. He would come back just as the sun began to sink, triumphantly bearing a dead thing on his back or empty-handed and dejected, his bow trailing in the dust behind him. In either case he would be difficult to talk to.

They had now decided that the main meal of the day was the last one you ate before it got dark, the one for which he provided the food (or not, as the case might be). In the morning they would eat cold meat and fruit. Later, they learned that you could obtain sustenance from animals without killing them and that you could make plants grow where you wanted them to grow. It became their fashion to begin the day with something milky and not with raw plants but with something made out of the plants. The two meals—the one at which you broke the fast that sleep enjoined and the one which you shared as the sun went down—gave a structure to their day, a sense of beginning and end. There was also a meal in the middle of the day but they seldom ate it together.

Much, much later, after the man and the woman had thickly populated the world with their progeny, the customs for the start of the day began to vary from time to time and from place to place. Some commenced with bread and an oatmeal porridge, but in those more numerous lands where rice was grown rather than wheat or oats, they preferred a watery rice gruel eaten with some strong-flavoured accompaniment like salt fish or eggs.

By now, the man had decided that the mysteries to which he was heir were so great that he must commune privately on the subject with men like himself. They would live together without women and make long, formal orations to the Old Man. By now, incidentally, they were reconciled with the Old Man. He had changed a lot since former times. Back then, He had thrown the man and the woman out of the garden because, like the pro He was, He knew a couple of potential rivals when He saw them. He knew that the serpent had been right when it told them that, if they chewed on the apple, they would be 'as gods, knowing good and evil,' and, sure enough, they'd done quite well for themselves. So He had sent word that their theft was forgiven, and, moreover, that they would be allowed to keep the loot.

Hence the formal orations, a constant stream of thank-you letters sent out by the men who lived together without women. For them the day was very rigidly structured: some hours were devoted to eating, some to working in the fields, others to talking to the Old Man. They rose at the eighth hour, while it was still dark, and said their prayers until the ninth hour, when together they sat down to bread and vegetables. Much later still, somebody invented a thing of metal and wood that was alive like a little animal and could tell you what hour of the day it was whenever you needed to know. Soon everybody's day was rigidly structured. The machines told you when to eat your meals, and, though there was no particular time at which you had to have breakfast, there was always a time by which breakfast had to be over and you about your work.

Unless, of course, you didn't have much work to speak of. By an amusing paradox, the age of the machine, of coal and steam and pistons, was for some the great age of breakfast. While many had to wake early to a scant meal or none at all and walk in darkness to drab factories, dilapidated shoes on their feet and festering resentment in their hearts, others rose to a varied and sumptuous board. On crisp European mornings during the hunting season, the man—who had never lost his love of killing the winged or four-footed beasts—would come down to a table laden with grilled pheasant, devilled kidneys, ragout, fish, fried eggs, sausages and bacon. There would be a side table with smoked hams, tongue, pressed meat, rolled goose, galantines and game pies. There would be preserves, quince jelly, toast, buns, brioches, marmalade and jam, bowls of rich cream with peaches and nectarines from the hothouse.

In warmer climes, where he sheared sheep all day and she never saw him for months on end, breakfast would be damper, fried salt pork and tea, consumed only after he had worked for two hours. It was followed by a lunch of damper, fried salt pork and tea. Supper was usually damper, fried salt pork and tea.

But the era of amplitude was drawing to a close. In the days of the pork chop and ale, or the later days of the devilled kidney, breakfast had been a leisurely meal—you would invite people to share it with you at your place or drop in on them while they breakfasted at theirs—but now the discipline of the machine ruled most lives and few had time for a long meal at the beginning of the day. Fortunately, the very industry which commanded them from their homes early each morning came to their assistance. All they had to do first thing was to pour out some corn, partly cooked, flavoured with barley malt and rolled flat into flakes. These were best eaten with milk as their sauce. Alternatively, there were grains of rice, cooked, allowed to dry and then puffed up under great pressure and at high temperature. The result was easier to eat if you poured milk on it. Or there were little biscuits made out of grains of wheat steamed and shredded. These were virtually inedible without milk.

Now the man no longer hunted—at least, not during the week—and the woman no longer had to stay at home tending to the fire or looking for fruits and berries. They both worked all day with many more of their kind in front of small screens, each of which afforded those who could read it far more knowledge than the Old Man had ever allowed them. But they had little time for breakfast, just a quick cup of coffee poured from a pot they put on before they went to the bathroom and gulped down on the way to the door. That and sometimes an apple.

# b is for boundary

Almost everything you need to know about boundaries you can learn from the closing scenes of Quentin Tarantino's film *Pulp Fiction*. Two hit persons, on their way back from a little matutinal rubbing out, have stopped at a coffee shop for some breakfast. They've settled into a booth and one of them is tucking into a big plateful of pork sausages and pancakes. The other has before him only a muffin and a cup of coffee. His colleague offers him a sausage but he declines it.

Why? Is he Jewish? No, he isn't Jewish, he just doesn't like swine. They're filthy: 'Pigs sleep and root in shit. That's a filthy animal. I don't wanna eat nothin' that ain't got sense enough to disregard its own faeces.'

So far, so good. The very booth at which they're sitting embodies an idea of boundaries. For the customer, it establishes an area that, for as long as he is a customer, is his particular area. At the same time, it has low walls, so that he can feel part of the general atmosphere of the place. And these two guys are having a conversation about boundaries that would not have surprised Rabbi Moses Maimonides, the great Jewish philosopher of the Middle Ages, who wrote that, 'The principal reason why the law forbids swine-flesh is to be found in the circumstance that its habits and food are very filthy and loathsome.'

But are pigs really more filthy and loathsome than, say, dogs? This is the question now raised in the coffee shop seminar. It is raised by the less intelligent of the two gunmen and it is not, of course, strictly relevant: his friend who doesn't eat pork doesn't eat dogs either, as he quickly points out.

Maybe not, but does he consider the dog, like the pig, to be a filthy animal? No, not filthy—dirty, certainly, though not filthy—but dogs have personality: 'And personality goes a long way.'

It does indeed. The pig (cruelly maligned in this matter) is held to be a filthy animal, and that's why we don't eat it. The dog is also held (rightly or wrongly) to be filthy, but that is not the reason why we don't eat it. We abstain from collie steak and Dalmatian burgers not because of the dog's lifestyle but because dogs have personality, and personality goes a long way; in fact, it makes the dog virtually a member of the family.

So would the guy who doesn't eat pig because it's filthy and doesn't think dogs are filthy because they've got personality eat dog if dogs didn't have personality? We never find out, but we do learn that, though a pig could, in principle, cease to be considered a filthy animal if it had personality, the odds are not encouraging: 'We'd have to be talkin' 'bout one charmin' motherfuckin' pig. I mean, he'd have to be ten times more charmin' than that Arnold on *Green Acres*. You know what I'm saying?'

Yes, I think we do, and I think that there's considerably more understanding of boundaries here than there is in a story we have from the eighteenth century about a certain Englishman who was very fond of pork. One day, it seems, this Englishman, happily tucking into a couple of chops, remarked to some friends that he wished he were Jewish. When they replied (as they were obviously meant to) that if he were Jewish he wouldn't be able to eat his favourite dish, he told them, no, he'd still be able to eat it, but he could have the pleasure of sinning at the same time.

Now there was a man who didn't understand boundaries. For him, the eating of pork was so natural that a law against it must have seemed like the dietary equivalent of a law against adultery: you can tell people to refrain and many of them will refrain, but not without the suspicion that it might perhaps be more fun to refrain from refraining. In fact, dietary laws don't seem to work like this at all: if you've been forbidden pork all your life, then the idea of eating it will as like as not be literally sickening to you. The American writer Diana Trilling speaks of a college friend of her husband's, a rabbi who abandoned his faith, broke with his family and underwent 'the dismal ritual of eating his first ham sandwich and vomiting'.

The fact is that we need boundaries, and not just because the breaking of them gives piquancy to life. We have a need to order our experience and, when it comes to food, that means distinguishing between what may be eaten and what may not, between where we may eat and where we may not, between those parts of the day that are devoted to eating and those that are not.

When we eat, we straddle the boundary that separates nature from culture. As animals, as children of nature, we need to eat, but our social being fills us with a need to transform our food through cooking into something that is as much cultural as natural. By cooking our food, we eat it in a way denied to other animals, thus emphasising to ourselves (though not, of course, to them) that our place in the order of things is very different to theirs.

This, surely, is why cannibalism is such a disturbing idea: to eat other people is to treat them like animals and thus to imply that we too might just be animals after all. For this reason, the act of cannibalism is never just a matter of gorging on the flesh of our fellow human beings: it is hedged about with ceremonies that establish its special status. This is why no ceremony has a more special status than the Roman Catholic Mass. In the twelfth century, the Church had to come up with some fairly fast thinking to answer those of its sons who said that in the Mass they literally crunched the body of Christ between their teeth. The result was the doctrine of transubstantiation, a drawing of boundaries so philosophical that it probably still puzzles the unreflecting faithful.

But no amount of philosophising can alter that fact that a human sacrifice is, to the Western mind, a terrible thing. There's an English poem from the Middle Ages in which Christ cries out from the cross about the unseemly way in which his body has been treated:

> Like a lambe led unto sacrefise,
> Slaine I was in most cruel wise.

The point about lambs led unto sacrifice is that the act of sacrificing them emphasises the boundary between us and the rest of the world. By treating the Son of God like a lamb, we put him on the wrong side of the boundary.

The ancient Greeks understood all this. It's true that when it came to the division of labour, they made rather fewer distinctions than we do—for them, the *mageiros*, the man who performed the sacrifice, who slaughtered the animal, was also the man who butchered the meat and then cooked it—but the end result was a neat drawing of boundaries. The *mageiros* was the link between a religious ritual of sacrifice and a social ritual of eating together. The latter ritual emphasised the boundary between the citizens who partook of it and everybody who hadn't been

*15*

invited. The former emphasised the boundary between mortals, who ate the meat, and the gods, who could get by on the smoke from the burning flesh as it ascended heavenwards.

But, most of all, the ritual emphasised the distinction between the sacrificer and the sacrificed, between humans and animals. The idea of animal rights would have seemed even more absurd to the Greeks than it does to me. For them, the animal world was one in which there was neither justice nor injustice, only violence. How could we have any social or political relationship with creatures so essentially unreasonable that they eat raw flesh and sometimes even each other? Wild animals are worst, of course, but domestic animals are just as dumb, though the fact that we are in control of their breeding gives them a slightly different status. The news that pigs have personality wouldn't have impressed Aristotle—not even Arnold in *Green Acres* would have impressed him—but he did believe that pigs and other domestic animals (oxen, sheep, goats) existed 'with a view to the good of man'. This was why they, and not hunted animals, could be used in acts of sacrifice.

In fact, domestic animals were so keen on helping humanity out that they actually consented to being sacrificed: they shook their heads from side to side, which in Greece signified assent. This, at least, was the fiction: in reality, the animal was provoked into this gesture when the sacrificer sprinkled its head with grain.

To us, of course, any sign that the animal consented to slaughter would be reason enough for not slaughtering it: if you can consent, you can think and if you can think, you're potentially a member of the family: personality goes a long way. The cast, or at least the menu, of Douglas Adams' science fiction novel *The Restaurant at the End of the Universe* features a talking bovine quadruped that has been bred up to want to be eaten. Not surprisingly, its very helpfulness ('I am the main Dish of the Day. May I interest you in parts of my body?') makes it an unappetising prospect for earthling diners: '"I just don't want to eat an animal that's standing there inviting me to," said Arthur, "it's heartless."'

Naturally, the Greeks knew as well as we do that if the animal understood what was going on during the sacrificial ceremony, it wouldn't be a very enthusiastic participant. For this reason, they did everything they could to soften the blow and to preserve the temple from the stench of the abattoir. There was nothing around that might lead the animal to expect death, and the stroke that killed it had to come as a surprise.

Human victims tended to be less obliging. In Aeschylus' tragedy *The Agamemnon*, we learn how Iphegenia—sacrificed by her father in order to secure favourable winds for his becalmed fleet—had to be gagged and held down on the altar lest she upset the ceremony. Her very struggles indicated that important boundaries had been transgressed. You don't sacrifice people, you don't sacrifice wild animals and you don't eat meat that hasn't been sacrificed.

Which brings us back to forbidden flesh and to pigs. 'Holiness means keeping distinct the categories of creation,' writes the anthropologist Mary Douglas. 'It therefore involves correct definition, discrimination and order.' In other words, holiness means knowing where the boundaries are and not trying to cross them. The problem with your pig is not that it's filthy but that, taxonomically speaking, it doesn't behave—or, at least, it doesn't behave if your taxonomy is that of the ancient Israelites—and this is reason enough for not eating it. To be holy, says Douglas, is to be whole, complete, free of imperfection. The Greeks, ever careful that their sacrificial rites should not be profaned by too much overt violence, would have agreed. This, sadly, is where the pig falls down. The ancient Israelites' idea of proper meat was flesh from the sort of animal that they were familiar with as pastoralists: sheep, cows and goats—cloven-hoofed cud-chewers. The pig has cloven feet but it doesn't chew the cud—it isn't a ruminant—and so it doesn't fit. It's unclean, inedible.

There are other possible explanations. Maimonides, who was a physician as well as a rabbi and a philosopher, believed that his people were forbidden pork because pork isn't good for you (an idea which proved to have considerable staying power: Giacomo Castelvetro, an Italian writer of the sixteenth century, gives a recipe for a sauce called *agliata*, made from walnuts, bread and garlic, which, he says, 'Prudent folk eat ... with fresh pork as an antidote to its harmful qualities ...'). Maimonides also favoured the idea that the object of Jewish dietary laws was to emphasise the boundary between the chosen people and their heathen neighbours. It's certainly true that food can often serve this purpose—there's a report from the 1940s of a Canadian farmer who believed in two basic food groups, 'fit to eat' and 'the Injuns ate that'—but in this case it wouldn't have worked, because the Israelites had neighbours who were equally suspicious of swine.

Mary Douglas has a more powerful opponent in the American anthropologist Marvin Harris. In pursuit of a less metaphysical account of swine-hating, Harris points out that in the Koran it is the pig alone, or almost alone, that is prohibited to the faithful. Unlike the Book of Leviticus, which classes all sort of foods as unclean—pigs, camels, shellfish, insects, eagles, ravens, ostriches and many other birds—the Koran has little to say about forbidden flesh. So why does it agree with Leviticus about swine? Harris has a materialist explanation.

Pigs, he tells us, are badly adapted to life in the Middle East. To thrive, they need shade and water—commodities that in this region are either expensive or troublesome to provide—and they feed best on roots and grains, food which could equally well be fed to humans. It's true that domestic pigs were raised in the Middle East in Biblical times, but their numbers fell off as more and more forest land, natural home of the pig, was destroyed to make room for crops or for grazing. You can't do much with a pig other than eat it—you can't keep it for its milk or as a beast of burden—so the pig became 'not only useless but worse than useless . . . a pariah animal'.

But what about the many other things that Jews are forbidden to eat? 'My point of departure,' says Harris, 'is that the food laws in Leviticus were mostly codifications of pre-existing food prejudices and avoidances.' For example, the forbidden seafood—clams, oysters and the like—were hardly the sort of thing that the inland-dwelling Israelites were likely to encounter. When it came to mammals, the Levite authorities, seeking some general rule to cover all available cases, hit upon the twin features of chewing the cud and parting the hoof. They thus excluded not only the pig but also the camel (which, in fact, doesn't chew the cud, though it looks as though it does).

It would be quite easy to square these two accounts: both depict the priestly authorities of ancient Israel as men who excelled at the drawing of fine boundaries. As the centuries passed, they got even better at it. Is a fish with an egg on it one dish or two? The Talmud has an answer: 'According to Beth Shammai it is considered as two dishes, but according to the school of Hillel it is considered only as one dish.' It adds, though, that the two schools agree that if you stuff your fish with a cooked egg, then you've definitely got two dishes; all of which is important when a festival falls on a Friday and you're faced with the necessity of preparing food both for the festival and for the Sabbath.

You can say that this anxious multiplying of distinctions, this drawing of boundaries with ever finer brushes, is the mark of a nervous culture desperately trying to keep a grip on its members and on the world in which they have to live; you can say (as I would) that you enjoy these sober, pedantic attempts to bring order to the chaos of human life: what you can't deny is that all this is about as unmodern as you can get. We do not worry whether a fish with an egg on it is one dish or two. Hell, we don't even worry whether a Big Mac eaten in the street at eleven in the morning is a late breakfast, an early lunch or neither of these things.

Dinner has disappeared in a welter of take-aways and microwaveable meals wrapped in plastic, breakfast is taken on the run, if at all, and the ideal lunch is the sort you can eat with one hand while the other keeps tapping at your computer keyboard. None of this is as recent as it looks: the great source of information about meal times, Arnold Palmer's book *Moveable Feasts*, traces the decline of set meals to the beginning of this century. Writing as long ago as 1952, Palmer concludes that, by his own time, 'day-long snacking, the flight of domestics, cafeteria service' have more or less done for any idea of a proper time at which to eat.

Palmer thought that the disappearance of set meal times was the culinary equivalent of mob rule, which must be a mistake: mobs may seem to behave erratically but a mob is a lot of people moving as one, whereas the decline of set meal times is the result of a lot of people moving like a lot of people. But there are limits to individualism, and most of us are happy to stay within them. What kind of breakfast is it where two people sit opposite each other, like Tarantino's mobsters, and eat entirely different things, sausages and pancakes for one, coffee and a muffin for the other? It may seem to be a breakfast where you can do what you like—and in a way it is—but, here as elsewhere, that which we like is that which falls within the boundary of the familiar: the four-seater booth with its formica-topped table, the menu, the conventions of service and of payment for service. This may not seem to be a world in which the boundaries are so tightly drawn that even the wilful transgression of them makes you want to throw up, but perhaps it is. We can't be sure, of course, but if someone were to take pork off the menu and replace it with dog, we might find out.

# C is for camel

Of all the animals that fall victim to our lust for fleshly protein, the camel is, I suspect, the least surprised to be eaten. Passive in its behaviour and supercilious in its look, the camel gives the distinct impression of hoping for little and expecting the worst. It has been eaten by the Chinese, the Persians and the Greeks, and by the Romans, who liked the heel most of all. Naturally the nations of the Middle East and North Africa specialise in its flesh; nowadays, indeed, the camel is more highly prized by them as a source of meat than as a beast of burden.

As far as I know, it was never among the riches of the East that were brought to Europe as the booty of empire, though on New Year's Day 1870, Parisians could buy camel from the English butcher's shop in the Boulevard Haussmann. The camel in question had been an inmate of the Paris Zoo, but the citizens, besieged by a Prussian army, had lost their interest in zoology and decided to put all manner of exotic animals to the cleaver. This famous act of betrayal was undertaken, I'm sure, with great reluctance, but I can never help imagining it as a sort of massacre of the innocents: a long parade of trusting, wide-eyed creatures, hopping, loping, lumbering and crawling their way to the abattoir behind those nice people who fed them every day and mopped out their cages. Pollux the elephant was perhaps the best-loved victim, and seems to have been the principal attraction in the shop, but there—'in the midst,' we're told, 'of nameless meats and unusual horns'—was a boy selling camel's kidneys.

As to the palatability of the meat ideas differ, but many are unfavourable:

> With a conceited air, contradictory and unpleasant, the camel arrives at 'souk el Khemis' in convoys. He occupies an important place in the market, blocks the streets of the Medina on his way down to the slaughter house and finishes up on the butcher's stall cut up in unappetizing violet coloured pieces destined as minced meat for 'Kefta'. The fat from the hump, white and sickly, cut out in huge thick petals decorates the stall and will be bought to make the 'khli' (preserved meat) of mutton, beef or camel. Less expensive, it can be cooked in the same way as beef, on a day when there is nothing else to be had, especially if the meat comes from a young camel.

These opinions are from a book called *Fez: Traditional Moroccan Cooking*, written by an author I know only as Z. Guinaudeau. To the ignorant reader, Mme. Guinaudeau's book has every appearance of being comprehensive—it tells you how to mix spices with hashish and how to barbecue lamb using the very freshest ingredients ('plunge the knife into the carotid and let the blood spurt out to the last drop')—so I'm prepared to interpret the general neglect of camel meat in her bourgeois pages as proof of its low status, at least in Fez.

In any case, it's the absence of camels that really interests me. There is not a single mention of them in the whole of the Koran, according to Jorge Luis Borges (who in turn cites Gibbon's *Decline and Fall of the Roman Empire*). Why should there be? The Koran was written by (or, as Muslims believe, dictated to) Mohammed, and he was an Arab, someone for whom camels were just part of the landscape. He had no reason to think of them as anything special, anything especially Arabian. As Borges remarks, 'if there were any doubt as to the authenticity of the Koran, this absence of camels would be sufficient to prove it is an Arabian work.' Only a falsifier, a tourist, a nationalist, someone with a point to make about what it is to be an Arab, would want to stuff a book like this full of camels. 'I think we Argentines can emulate Mohammed, can believe in the possibility of being Argentine without abounding in local colour,' says Borges, clinching his argument that it is possible to be a truly Argentine writer without writing about gauchos.

This is an argument worth considering when we ask ourselves (as apparently we must) whether there's such a thing as an Australian cuisine. Borges should help us resist the temptation to think that what might be Australian about an Australian cuisine would have to be its use of Australia's equivalents of the camel: the kangaroo, the emu and the rest of that vast, anomalous array of flora and fauna that so bemused the first white explorers of this island.

There is, of course, much to be said for the lean meat and nutritious vegetation that Australia's first inhabitants enjoyed. 'It's a kind of myth that a lot of people hold that Aboriginal people lived some kind of hand-to-mouth existence,' said a nutritionist at the University of Sydney, fresh from the study of fifteen thousand indigenous foods. 'But the evidence is quite clear that their lifestyle as hunter-gatherers was what people now call the original affluent lifestyle. They didn't have to spend all day collecting food. They had many more hours of leisure than we do, and, as a result, they had a very rich cultural and ceremonial life.'

In the circumstances, that aspect of their cultural life that had to do with food could hardly be other than an Australian cuisine, prepared as it was by Australians with uniquely Australian ingredients. Moreover, it's difficult to imagine any real cuisine—any style of producing, preparing and eating food—that did not use what was available locally. But it would be absurd to think that the cuisine of a particular locality should restrict itself to ingredients peculiar to that locality.

In the 1950s, Roland Barthes had a go at identifying the culinary symbols of Frenchness. He decided that there was wine and there was steak and chips. Wine, said Barthes, present at all the ceremonials of French life, helped to mark out the social environment. It was felt by the French to be as much a national possession as their 360 varieties of cheese. Steak, imparting to those who ate it a 'bull-like strength', was the same. It was 'a part of all the rhythms, that of the comfortable bourgeois meal and that of the bachelor's bohemian snack.'

But what is peculiarly French about wine and steak? Don't other nations have grapes as red as those of France, or bulls as full-blooded? They do, though, to give Barthes his due, their symbolic function may be different in these other places.

Steak, for example. 'In it,' writes Barthes, 'blood is visible, natural, dense, at once compact and sectile.' Not here it isn't. In Australia, the rightful place for a steak is the barbecue, and the sovereign natural force at the barbecue is not blood but the fire which evaporates blood and renders meat anything but sectile. Indeed, Australians in search of their national cuisine need perhaps look no further than their own backyards. Of course, the barbecue is no more a uniquely Australian phenomenon than the steak is uniquely French, but the barbecue in

Australia has, like steak in France, been naturalised and appropriated as a national symbol. I'm not sure, though, that Borges would have been very impressed. What he has to say is directed not just against the clumsy use of peculiar local fauna as a symbol of nationhood but against any reductive nationalism at all. After all, nationalism of this kind, gathering up and treasuring every local peculiarity of customs and manners, is a very recent phenomenon.

It has always been recognised that different peoples chose and prepare their food in different ways, and even chew it in different ways: 'The Germans chew with the mouth closed, and find it ugly to do otherwise,' says a French writer of the sixteenth century. 'The French, on the other hand, half open the mouth, and find the procedure of the Germans rather dirty.' Not until the nineteenth century did it occur to anybody that all these little local quirks might be things of unique value. This was when the intelligentsia decided that there was such a thing as a national spirit, that the peasantry were its true custodians and that its true emblem was whatever sad array of dirndls, ribbons, embroidered waistcoats and silly hats the peasants wore on high days and holidays.

Over the last two centuries, nationalism has found eloquent expression in war, genocide and the tourist industry. As things have turned out, though, war and genocide are more truly expressive of the nationalist spirit than tourism or the encouragement of tourism can be. Tourists want distraction, they want variety, as much of it as possible, and variety is furnished most richly in nations animated not by a monolithic sense of nationhood but by a vigorous regionalism. Italy, a country less than one twenty-fifth the size of Australia, is a tightly packed box filled with regional delights you've either forgotten about or, more likely, never knew were there in the first place: *N'docca n'docca*, the near-unpronounceable pork casserole of the Abruzzi; the thirteen-course feast that the Molisani eat on St Joseph's day; the dish of raw vegetables they give you in Puglia halfway through a meal and which they call *lo pintone*, 'the push', because it's supposed to push down the earlier courses and make room for more— these are only a few of the pleasures available in only a part of the country.

In the first flush of Italian unification, Pellegrino Artusi wrote his country's most famous cookery book out of a desire to do away with all this noisy regionalism and replace it with a truly national cuisine. He failed—if Italian cuisine is becoming less regional these days, it's largely because the pasta of the south is quicker and easier to prepare than the rice and polenta of the north—but at least he was proceeding in a rational direction. It is rational (perhaps a bit too coldly rational) to believe that regional differences can be ironed out, but is it rational to think that these wrinkles in the nation's fabric can be put in just because you happen to want them? Is a regional cuisine really the sort of thing that you can start to create or is it not rather something that you wake up one morning and notice that you've had all along?

Australian regionalists can take pleasure in the Barossa Valley, which Maggie Beer describes as 'the one place in Australia where there is a strong peasant culture and food heritage.' United by the German language and their Lutheran faith, the first settlers of the Barossa formed a distinct community of small landowners. The food they produced was primarily for themselves and their own families, so they cared about its quality.

This seems to be the most important aspect of regionalism: in essence, it's not about quaint local customs or religious festivals, it's about producing food for your own consumption. And this, perhaps, is why we don't have genuine culinary regionalism in this country. 'We're looking historically at a situation where the producer of the food never became the eater of the food,' said the distinguished Australian cook Phillip Searle when I asked him about regionalism. 'He was always the person who saw the food that he produced in terms of money, rather than in terms of its enjoyment or lore or whatever.' Australian agriculture, in other words, has usually been a form of extractive industry, carried out on a large scale and with a view to exports. It has seldom been a matter of small farmers working their own patch, feeding just themselves and their families.

Phillip Searle believes that the new regionalism—so fashionable lately in Australian food chat—can never be a true regionalism. All it amounts to is a celebration of local produce, the particular shelf full of good things turned out by, say, the Riverina, the Orange District or King Island. A few years ago, the organisers of the 'Food of the Orange District' festival invited Phillip Searle to cook for them. He turned up with his knives and his kitchen staff, gave the local produce the once-over, liked it and, by all accounts, did great things with it. Nothing wrong with that, but it's not regionalism. Regionalism has nothing to do with guest chefs and everything to do with making the best of what you've got. *N'docca n'docca* was not invented by a star chef on loan from a restaurant in Milan.

As Phillip Searle sees it, the new regionalism, centred on products and not on home cooking, inverts the traditional relationship between raw material and dish: 'Regionalism is based first of all on a product that's unique to the area,' he says, 'but, more so, it's based on the accumulation of dishes around that product, and that will never happen here.'

Perhaps we should not want it to happen here. The regionalist spirit, like the nationalist spirit, fills the mind with phantasms. Nationalists and regionalists are always grabbing at the air in front of them, hoping that this time, just once, the beautiful vision before their eyes will turn out to be solid. Tourists are encouraged to do the same thing, though their commitment to the vision is usually only temporary. 'Authenticity' is one of the more recent buzz words in the tourism business, and the love of authenticity—in a world where most experience comes vacuum-packed and brightly labelled—sends travellers out in search of distant places, unspoilt landscapes, peasant cuisines. The result, I suspect, is that many an industrious villager, from Vietnam to the Algarve, has been hurt by the reproachful glances of tourists disappointed to find that the famous traditional local dish is no longer done in the traditional time-consuming way.

You wouldn't think so to read some cookery books and most guide books, but the fact is that societies change. People no longer work in the fields, woman can no longer spend all day watching over a cooking pot. Claudia Roden—born in Cairo, resident in London—is a food writer who understands these things. 'Why,' she once asked me, 'should my readers on the other side of the world spend two hours doing something that, in the country of the dish, they don't do any more?' She knows that Moroccan houses—even houses with as many as six cooks—use packet couscous, so she's not going to force anybody who doesn't live in Morocco to go out and buy the original grain. Her book on Italian food even permits stock cubes.

This seems sensible. Authenticity, elusive enough when pursued across deserts or amongst palms and pines, is hardly likely to be run to earth by anybody who just stays at home with a good cookery book and an array of stainless-steel kitchen implements. The late Jane

Grigson—a wonderful food writer, who certainly knew authenticity when she tasted it—told me that she'd once nervously cooked a French meal in London for a visiting French gastronome. He enjoyed it, and afterwards told her that he hadn't realised English food could be so good. And if Jane Grigson, who'd been to France and knew what French food was supposed to taste like, couldn't fool a Frenchman, how could I possibly hope to fool a Moroccan with my book in one hand and my bag of genuine, uncooked couscous in the other? The best I could manage would probably seem to the Moroccan rather like a blurred photo of a loved one.

But, if I can't make it to Morocco, won't I get some idea of what the food there tastes like by going to a Moroccan restaurant or, if I'm lucky, a Moroccan home in Sydney? This is a difficult question. One answer is that Moroccan food isn't necessarily just the food they eat in Morocco. 'There is also a cuisine of people who have migrated,' said Claudia Roden. 'Migrants always change their food. They change it in their home according to what they have available.'

And it's not just ingredients that change: people can find themselves doing jobs in the new country that it would never have occurred to them to do in the old one. Take Greek restaurants in Australia. Are they authentic, with their entrees of taramasalata, tzaziki and humous followed by a lot of grilled dead flesh and a very small salad? 'No, not at all,' I was told by Ireni Germanos, a restaurateur from South Australia. 'You see, in Australia men cook and they don't know how. Men in Greece don't cook.' The implication seems to be that Greek men, knowing nothing of the skills required of a cook but in need of a job, have foisted burnt meat on an Australian public ignorant of what Greek food is supposed to taste like.

Not having been to Greece, I can't say how accurate this claim is, though I wonder whether what we should deplore is not the unauthenticity of the menu but its frequent lack of anything that makes food interesting. When I used to sit down to eat at Ali Akbar in Hobart (now, sadly, no longer with us), I would do so in expectation of the greatest gastronomic pleasure, untroubled by speculations as to whether this was an authentic Lebanese experience or even an authentic Lebanese-Australian experience. If Ali Akbar had not been what we call an ethnic restaurant, the question of authenticity would never have arisen.

A menu in Sydney recently offered me something described as 'Cajun salmon' on a bed of udon noodles. I did not bother to find out, but I suspect that, in this context, 'Cajun' just means 'burnt', and, for all I know to the contrary, burnt salmon may go very well with the flavour and texture of udon noodles; but you don't have to come from Yokohama or the Louisiana Bayous to realise that, whatever the virtues of the dish, its description is gastronomically illiterate. Nobody complains, though, that this sort of thing is unauthentic, because the restaurant in question is not some unassuming suburban eatery with tourist posters on the wall but a well-appointed establishment in an expensive part of town offering food that is eclectic, exciting, adventurous. Only ethnic restaurants are assumed to have a closed, unvarying repertoire.

George Haddad, owner of Ali Akbar, played the orthodox Lebanese restaurant repertoire for about two years, but then something happened. Singing the old songs (as he puts it) just got boring, and not merely boring but frustrating as well. Here they were, surrounded by superb produce but apparently precluded from using it. 'We're in Tasmania, we have fresh salmon,' George told me. 'So I can't use it, because I'm running a Middle Eastern restaurant? Well, it's not good enough. So I wondered: if the salmon had ventured up the Mediterranean, what would my predecessors have done? Of course, they would have used it. So then our job was to produce the salmon with unmistakable Middle Eastern flavours, which we do.'

Much of what is best about Australian restaurant culture was created by migrants of the mind, people who discovered overseas a culinary inspiration that they couldn't find at home. Their approach has been that of the highly intelligent newcomer, swotting up on the history and traditions of the new country and coming to know them better than most of the locals. But there are also cooks who've journeyed in the other direction, and

George Haddad is one of them. He was born in Lebanon—he came to Australia in 1967, when he was just sixteen—but his food has a second-generation feel. It respects the flavours of the old country but without cankerous nostalgia. Authentically reflecting an aspect of migrant experience, it manages at once to be Australian and Middle Eastern, and to achieve this synthesis without the aid of kangaroos or camels.

# d is for delusion

This is an absolutely true story. I didn't see it happen myself, but I heard about it from a guy who said that the friend who told it to him swore it was true. There are these four American cops, you see, and they're big, real big. I mean, we're talking the stuff of TV legend here: straining buttons, great blue swags obscuring the gun belt, and sweat, buckets of sweat. They roll into a pizza place and lever themselves into a booth. They're just lighting up when the waitress comes over to take their order. They go for the mega-pizzas, four of them, heavy on the mozzarella with some ham and peperoni, no salad, of course, and to follow maybe a double order each of ice cream.

'You want beers with that?' asks the waitress.

'Hell no,' says a cop, 'we want red wine—we've got to think of our health.'

The best news that guys like this ever heard was that

red wine might be good for you. It was delivered to them, no doubt via TV, in the form of what is now widely known as 'the French paradox'. The paradox is this: the French diet is high in saturated fats—the bad sort of fat, the kind that's supposed to push up your cholesterol level—but, when it comes to rates of coronary heart disease, the French are almost as healthy as the notoriously fit Japanese. Research into the reason for this has singled out the possibility that the French metabolism is sustained in health by regular doses of wine. (Experimental work in the laboratory confirms that alcohol, if consumed in moderation, reduces dangerous stickiness of the blood platelets and increases the HDL cholesterol, the 'good' cholesterol which carries away fat from the arteries.) Now, the nice thing about this is that it doesn't look like you're being asked to give up anything. We've all dreamt of being able to eat as much as we like of whatever we like and then just to be able to take a pill to make everything all right again. Well, here was that pill and, hey, it was a couple of glasses of red wine—no shit.

Need I say that it doesn't work like this? That you can't just add red wine to your usual diet and hope to live forever? There are many differences between what Americans eat and what the French eat—many differences, too, in the circumstances in which it is eaten—and research has yet to tell us which differences are relevant and which are not. There is one difference, though, that seems to me to be paramount: the French enjoy food and the Americans don't. Sure, the Americans eat a lot, and presumably derive some enjoyment from what they eat, but there is a desperate, obsessive, love-hate quality to their relationship with food.

Of course, the Americans and the French are merely the opposite ends of a continuum. The Americans are not alone in wanting to know how to stop ice cream losing its creamy flavour when its fat content has been reduced, how to make a low-fat cheese that isn't rubbery, how to keep cakes made with polydextrose instead of sugar from shrinking, sinking and going dark. Perhaps the French are not alone in their well-attested lack of interest in these things (one can't imagine the Chinese being very charmed by them, either). Sugar substitutes and salt substitutes are all very well if the products to which they are added were never very subtle in the first place. The French, however, don't want the instant hit of flavour that these products furnish; they want subtlety and nuance and would rather eat less of a real thing than lots of an imitation.

American food (and much of ours) is essentially a matter of the feints and disguises with which a guilty mind tries to delude itself. A little while ago, American food journalists got very excited about what they called a 'guilt-free meat'. Now, one might have supposed that with regard to the eating of meat, the only possible occasion of guilt would be the fact that it necessitates the slaughtering of a fellow creature; if you're cool about that, then everything else ought to be easy. But, no, this meat is guilt-free because it is tender, low in fat, calories and cholesterol, free-range and free of steroids and hormones, with a nutritional profile similar to those of salmon and skinless chicken.

Unfortunately, the meat in question is New Zealand venison, and venison is a difficult thing to sell to Americans, who tend to think that eating venison means eating Bambi (though that, I can't help thinking, would be no bad thing). In this they differ markedly from the Germans, who are accustomed to eating venison during the hunting season and whose view of it is much more robust than the American but equally unrealistic. Whereas the Americans don't like to think that they're chewing on doe-eyed cartoon characters, the Germans positively relish the idea that they're enjoying something that was alive very recently and has been brought to them on the back of some beefy forester in lederhosen and a hat with a feather in it. They're wrong, of course: a large proportion of the venison they eat is farmed and imported from New Zealand. In America, the lack of strong flavour in New Zealand venison is a great asset: in Germany, it isn't, so chefs hold their venison a little while in order to give it that gamy, *Der Freischütz* feel.

Both the Germans and the Americans are deluding themselves, but it is difficult not to think that the German delusion is the healthier of the two. The German delusion, though quaint, is founded on a desire for strong flavours. The American delusion is founded on denial and a desire for escape: denial that meat means slaughter and escape from the consequences of stuffing large quantities of it into your body. I don't know who will live longer or who will be happier, your average fat German or your average fat American, but I do know that red wine goes better with pizza than beer does. So perhaps we should just be thankful that the new delusions taste better than the old ones.

# e is for exotic

It's possible that there are still some undiscovered tribes in the world. It's possible but unlikely, and we can probably assume that anyone who's undiscovered at this late stage in the game just isn't interested in being discovered. In any case, why do we (or some of us) want there to be such people? Why were the media so excited a few years ago when a group of Aborigines—untouched, we were told, by white civilisation—came in from the desert?

Perhaps it has something to do with the appealing idea that there might be people who are so near to us and yet so far from us: so physically close that they are almost amongst us, yet psychologically so remote that they don't even know we exist.

And, being uncontaminated by us, they are perfectly, completely, themselves. It's fantasy, of course: the Aborigines in question knew about white society and had chosen, for their own good reasons, to come in.

But if you're looking for an undiscovered tribe—or at least an uncontaminated tribe—romantic imagination can offer you a far wider field to choose from than just Antipodean hunter-gatherers. You might like to try these people:

> mixing little with the modern world, they earn a living by fishing, boating, trapping, and by selling handwoven baskets and cloth. In a region of few roads, they live on simple wooden houseboats, dependent on the waterways and the pirogue ...

The harmless rustics depicted here are in fact citizens of the United States. They're the Cajun people of Southwest Louisiana, and this imaginative description of them comes from *The American Heritage Book of Great Historic Places*, which was published in 1973.

In the real world Cajuns are so far from being an undiscovered tribe of simple swamp dwellers that, even as this fantasy was being concocted, they were making attempts to preserve a culture that they perceived as being in danger. The threats were both cultural and economic. The Cajuns had been living in Louisiana since the second half of the eighteenth century, when they had arrived there after being exiled by the British government from their native Acadia, which the British insisted on calling Nova Scotia (the word 'Cajun' is an Anglophone attempt at *Acadiens* or *Cadiens*).

Even at this very early period of their history they were not totally remote from their neighbours: they had many dealings with them, they married some of them, they even married some of the French Creoles, who had been living in Louisiana for most of the century and liked to think of themselves as something of an aristocracy, more than a cut above the newly arrived peasants. But the Cajuns remained a distinct, French-speaking community until the twentieth century, when a number of developments threatened their autonomy: legislation that forbade the use in public schools of any language but English; the discovery of oil in Louisiana, which brought in outsiders and salaried jobs; improvements in transport and the growth of mass media.

The culture was threatened but by no means extinct; it still had enough vitality for the hope of renewal to be a realistic one. This was the context in which the Council for the Development of French in Louisiana was founded (and this happened, incidentally, five years before *The American Heritage Book of Great Historic Places* painted for the American public its picture of remote rusticity).

In fact, though, what was in store for Cajun culture was a fate more complex than either inundation or preservation in the folklorist's aspic, and food was much implicated in what happened next.

In its origins, Cajun cuisine is the cuisine of a poor

people who have adapted brilliantly to circumstances. Gumbo, the dish most associated with them, shares at least four principal characteristics with many of the peasant foods of the world: it is a kind of stew or thick soup, it uses only one pot, it has a very long cooking time, and it's the sort of dish in which the cook can make do with whatever ingredients happen to be available: fish, fowl, game or domestic meats. Cajuns were described as eaters of gumbo at least as early as 1803, but the very name of the dish tells us that its origins lie a long way from Louisiana. *Guingombo* is a West African word for okra, and okra, which becomes stringy and sticky when cooked, is the principal thickening agent in many gumbos. A gumbo thus thickened is called a *gumbo fevi*: the more famous *gumbo filé*—famous if only because of Fats Domino—dispenses with okra in favour of French methods and native American ingredients.

Gumbo is based on a roux, not the white roux of classical French cuisine, but a roux formed by browning flour in oil or fat and cooking almost until it burns. Just before the gumbo is served, it can be thickened (though this isn't compulsory) with filé powder: the leaves of the sassafras plant dried, pounded and then sieved, originally by the Choctaw Indians. It's always eaten with rice, which was introduced to Louisiana by the French and later grown by German and Anglo-American farmers who migrated there from the Midwest in the nineteenth century.

So gumbo is already a dish of agreeably mixed ancestry: an exotic dish both literally, in that it employs ingredients exotic to its region, and in the more colloquial sense of the word. But there is one other ingredient, an optional extra, that, more probably than anything else, characterises Cajun food for many people outside Louisiana (and perhaps even for quite a few who live there). I'm talking about cayenne pepper, a Spanish and Afro-Caribbean embellishment, and I'm talking about deep heat, because Cajun food is hot. Or, rather it's been hot for the last forty years or so and really hot for the last ten.

Today, Cajuns like to think of themselves as a people of cast-iron stomachs, but older Cajuns, it seems, agree that hot seasoning was never an integral part of Cajun cooking. Things seem to have hotted up in the 1940s and 1950s, perhaps because women started smoking and, with their tastebuds thus compromised, turned to the highly-seasoned dishes that the men used to cook on their hunting trips. For whatever reason, Cajun food was certainly way hot during the childhood of the man who was eventually to take it all round the world. 'I remember when I was a kid,' he says, 'sometimes it was so hot it would make your head itch, you know, give you hiccups.' He does add that what he remembers is not just heat but flavour. It is heat, though, that most people associate with his food.

The man in question is Paul Prudhomme: mountainous chef, owner of restaurants in New Orleans and New

York, TV star, author of several cookery books and the figure behind a range of ready-mixed, spicy products that can be found even on the shelves of Australian delis and supermarkets. There's no doubt that Prudhomme is a very fine cook and a very good marketing man; there's no doubt that he's the person responsible for the fashionability of Cajun food in the late 1980s. Equally, there's little doubt that he's the person most responsible for the popular conception of Cajun cuisine as something that blows the top of your head off.

By the '80s, Cajun food was ready for marketing. It had picturesque and exotic associations, thanks to sources of misinformation like *The American Heritage Book of Great Historic Places*, and now, courtesy of Paul Prudhomme and others, it had a single, easily grasped characteristic: it was really, really hot.

There was one other thing it needed, though, and that was a tourist centre with which it could be linked. It found one in a town that had never before been associated with Cajun culture, a town in which the word 'Cajun', like the word 'coonass', had often been a term of abuse: New Orleans. Go to New Orleans now and you'll find the word 'Cajun' fairly indiscriminately attached to anything saleable and particularly anything that can be reasonably described as hot, whether that heat is brought on by cayenne pepper, the weather or sex. This development reached a sort of apogee in the 1987 movie *The Big Easy*, in which Dennis Quaid struggles with his vowel sounds as a Cajun cop in the New Orleans Police Department—itself an implausible idea—and takes Ellen Barkin for some gumbo at Tipitina's. (Incidentally, Tipitina's is a night club and, at the time the film was made, you couldn't get food there, though you can certainly get it now.) But at least New Orleans can't be blamed for Cajun beer. This, apparently, is brewed in Milwaukee—according to the traditional Cajun method, it says on the label—and what makes it Cajun is the fact that it contains cayenne pepper.

Of course, New Orleans has a perfectly good cuisine of its own, at least as interesting as Cajun and every bit as various in its origins. This is Creole food—a genuine high cuisine, served in restaurants and great houses—which has been fashionable in New Orleans for a century or more. Creole food went through its own period of revival long before Cajun. At the beginning of the century, the local paper, *The Picayune*, published a cookbook with the intention of preserving a tradition that was felt by the authors to be in danger now that the Civil War and the emancipation of the slaves had led to 'the passing of the faithful old negro cooks—the "mammies", who felt it a pride and honour, even in poverty, to cling to the fortunes of their former masters and mistresses, and out of the scant family allowance to be still able to prepare for their "ole Miss'" table a "ragout" from a piece of neck meat, or a "pot-au-poivre" from many mixtures that might grace the table of a king.'

Creole food shares a number of characteristics with Cajun food, and has done so especially since the 1930s, when the publication in local papers in Cajun country of extracts from the *Picayune Cook Book* led to a melding of the two cuisines. In particular, they have in common at least two dishes, jambolaya (a rice-based dish related to the Spanish paella) and gumbo. You've always been able to get gumbo in all the best places in New Orleans. At a banquet held there in 1803, twenty-four different sorts of gumbo were served, and the *Picayune Cook Book* gives recipes for nine varieties, 'gathered with care,' it tells us, 'from the best Creole housekeepers of New Orleans, ... handed down from generation to generation by the old negro cooks, and preserved in all their delightful combinations by their white Creole mistresses.' Today, gumbo appears on the menu at Antoine's, the oldest and best-known restaurant in New Orleans. It's listed along with the soups—or '*potages*', because this menu is in French—and it's described there as 'creole gumbo', which makes it look something like an exotic import.

Now, because Creole cuisine is, among other things, a cuisine of restaurants and great houses, a New Orleans gumbo is very different from a Cajun gumbo. Some Cajuns say that a gumbo with tomatoes in it is a New Orleans gumbo, but the real difference is that in New Orleans the cooking times are much shorter; the recipes in the *Picayune* book will give you a gumbo in under two hours, whereas you can need about six for a

Cajun gumbo and some can take all day. Mathé Allain, a teacher at the University of Southwestern Louisiana, French but married to a Cajun, told me that she thought the reason for the shorter cooking time was that the urban cook did not, like her rural counterpart, need to be able to leave the pot in the fire for a long time while she attended to other chores. Of course, the longer cooking time of the rural version—which is typical of many Cajun dishes, not just of gumbo—also enables you to make use of older and tougher meat, but Mme Allain was uncompromising when I asked her whether you should shorten the time if your chook isn't all that tough. That would be disastrous, she told me: 'Just look for a rooster that has caused a lot of trouble for many years in the chicken yard.' I'm still looking, and those few words of hers sum up for me as much as anything else the difference between a rural and an urban cuisine. (I cook gumbo at home, but it's always Creole gumbo.)

Almost any attempt to take a rural or poor cuisine into the restaurant world will have to tackle one central challenge: the brown goo problem. An awful lot of people in this world—poor people, people who work on the land—eat brown goo. Some eat highly-seasoned brown goo, some eat bland brown goo; some eat their brown goo with their hands, some use spoons; some eat the same brown goo every day, some work hard to vary the brownness or the gooiness of what they eat. Stewed dishes cooked a long time are the basis of domestic cuisines in

China, the Middle East, North Africa, the poorer parts of Europe and in many other places. They often taste very good, these goos, but they don't usually look very pretty, which is a problem because we expect our restaurant food to be photogenic. What tends to happen, then, is that the peasant dish gets dolled up; it's not allowed into polite society until it has put on its Sunday best.

There's quite a tradition of this sort of thing: at the beginning of the century, as Elizabeth David points out, the great French chef Escoffier did it often and with considerable panache. Faced with a dish from his native Provence—sliced potatoes with artichokes, baked with olive oil and garlic, and scented with wild thyme—he replaced the garlic with truffle and the olive oil with butter, then used this vegetable dish as a basis for a cut of spring lamb, because he was working for people who wouldn't dream of a main course without meat.

It's less easy to do anything about the long cooking times which make many peasant dishes quite unsuitable for restaurants. This is a point not lost on the chefs of New Orleans. A few years ago, Raymond Thomas Snr, head chef at the French Market Seafood House, pointed out that a home gumbo was different from a restaurant gumbo. A home gumbo didn't have to look good, so you didn't need to bother straining the seasoning, and you could use tasty but unbeautiful ingredients, like the backs and feet of chicken. But his chief point was that you could let a home gumbo set for two or three days to bring it to the peak of its flavour. 'That's when gumbo is really gumbo,' he said. Even Paul Prudhomme, marketing man that he is, recognises that you can't do Cajun cooking anywhere but in Louisiana and that you can't really do it in a restaurant. His solution seems to be to transform the long-cooked foundation of the dish into a sauce which can be cooked in advance for an appropriately long time and then added when it's needed.

I've tasted the result and it's very good. You'd have to be a harsh critic to condemn it as a travesty of Cajun cuisine. How can it be a travesty? The ingredients are the same and the cook is a Cajun.

Of course, Paul Prudhomme is not just a Cajun who happens to be a cook: he's a Cajun cook, and his Cajun identity—which he himself has helped define with copious shakings of cayenne pepper—is essential to his identity as a cook and as a marketable product. He is as far as it is possible to be from the shy, unspoilt rustics whose gaze is reluctant to meet ours in the pages of *The American Heritage Book of Great Historic Places*.

Algazzali, a medieval Islamic philosopher, says somewhere that the only true traditionalist is the man who doesn't know that he is a traditionalist. To choose to be a traditionalist, to single this out among a variety of options, is to wear tradition like a coat that may be put on and taken off at will. But the true traditionalist can't choose to be a traditionalist, because tradition has defined for him what he will see and therefore what he can choose. Barry Jean Ancelet, a Cajun academic and folklorist, recently asked a local musician whether he was sorry that Cajuns had been discovered. 'I'm even sorrier that Cajuns have discovered themselves,' said the musician. Discovering yourself means being self-conscious about your traditions; it means being exotic to others, and perhaps even to yourself.

The others will, of course, have their own idea about where the exotic is to be met with. Cajun music—whose home is the timber-floored dance hall—is met with at concerts and on CDs. Cajun food, an essentially domestic cuisine, is met with in restaurants far from the bayous, far from Louisiana, far, even, from any state of the Union. 'You didn't hear so much about Cajun when we were young,' said an elderly Cajun woman. 'We were just old-fashioned, country people. It wasn't a big deal like it is now.' But being exotic is, in its very essence, a big deal.

# f is for fire

I love the smell of carcinogens in the morning: the smoke rising as the grey of the charcoal begins to glint with red; the pink, viscous flesh, brief host to flies while it awaits its incineration; those plastic ranks of sauce bottles, all gummy at the nozzle.

The barbecue is the only place where we are truly aware of the fire that cooks our food. The blue gas jets of the domestic kitchen, its glowing electric rings, its incomprehensible microwaves—none of them seems to have much to do with the basic, elemental power of fire. Even the gas barbecue seems more basic than any of these. The jet is the same cold, unwelcoming sapphire that we see in the kitchen, but here— with no paintwork to be spared from stains—there's nothing to force the cook to turn down the flame. He can allow the meat to sizzle and burn and smoke.

And, yes, of course the cook is a he, because cooking *en plein air* over an open fire is nowadays largely a male performance; it recalls the world of our hunting fathers. 'A male cook is likely to concentrate his efforts on meat or seafood main dishes,' says the anthropologist C. Paige Gutierrez, writing of the barbecue in Cajun society, though she could equally well be writing of the rest of America or of Australia. 'Items acquired directly from the environment, such as game or fresh fish, are strongly associated with men's cooking.' So at the end of the twentieth century, fire has reverted to being what it was at the beginning of our journey, in the mythic past: a masculine possession, stolen from the gods by impudent men. (Actually, stories of the theft of fire—whether the thief be male, female or animal—are at least easier to grasp than the idea that some prehistoric genius actually invented firemaking. As the French philosopher Gaston Bachelard points out, it is very difficult to imagine how anybody could have hit on the notion that rubbing two sticks together would enable you to mimic the power of lightning. Why would you try it in the first place? And if you didn't know what was coming, wouldn't boredom set in long before ignition occurred?)

Flame has not, of course, been banished from our lives—it's still possible to enjoy an open fire in winter—but our idea of the heat that cooks has become separated from our idea of the warmth that comforts. The fire at the barbecue is fierce and masculine. Men are in charge of it and it has nothing to do with nurturing, female warmth.

But this separation, which even now is not complete, is of comparatively recent origin. Bachelard writes touchingly of his grandmother's kitchen. The scene is rural France towards the end of the nineteenth century and the infant Bachelard, son and grandson of cobblers, enjoys a fresh egg cooked under the ashes of the fire. His grandmother rekindles the flames by puffing her cheeks and blowing into a steel tube. 'Everything,' writes the grown-up philosopher, 'would be cooking at the same time: the potatoes for the pigs, the choice potatoes for the family.' If he has been good, they will bring out the waffle iron. Eating the waffles, golden and crackling, is like eating fire itself. The pigs, as we've been told, are being fed as well, but this doesn't alter the fact that the grandmaternal hearth so nostalgically evoked isn't just a place of utilitarian heat. It is also a place of comfort, nurture and, as Bachelard puts it, reverie.

Peasant kitchens like this were such comforting and secure places because they were so clearly defined by the heat they contained and the walls that contained it. But even without walls, fire itself can define a nurturing space. Hunter-gatherers, returning to the campsite at the end of the day with their burdens of fruit and dead flesh, knew that home was the fire that cooked their food. You sit around the fire and the light of the flames turns whatever is behind you into a particularly black black wall.

Home is what you can see by the fire's light; whatever is beyond is foreign. 'This their place of dwelling was only a fire,' said William Dampier of the Australian Aborigines he saw at the end of the seventeenth century. Later observers noticed that wherever and whenever Aborigines stopped, they lit a small fire: the focus of family life, the centre of ritual. Fire is a tool that domesticates those who use it.

This idea that cooking with fire has something very essential to do with civilisation is developed at length, and with notorious ingenuity, by the French anthropologist Claude Lévi-Strauss. If you don't cook but you do eat meat, what sort of meat can you eat? You can eat raw meat, which puts you on a par with carnivorous animals, or you can eat rotten meat, which earns you the status of carrion-eating animals. But once you decide to cook your meat, you leave the animal world and become truly human. Lévi-Strauss looks at the myths of a number of South American Indian tribes and concludes: 'not only does cooking mark the transition from nature to culture, but through it and by means of it, the human state can be defined with all its attributes, even those that, like mortality, might seem to be the most unquestionably natural.' Mortality is the lot of human kind: in these myths, the moment when fire is mastered and cooking becomes possible is the moment when people become human and, consequently, mortal. To taste cooked food is to taste your own death.

But, on the other hand, cooking is now so much part of our humanity that to taste cooked food—game, fish, an egg, a waffle—is to taste something so comforting that it may offer solace even in the face of mortality. Every now and then, you read in the papers that some state of the Union where people are still judicially fried or poisoned has sentenced somebody to death. Accounts dwell on the protracted process of appeal, the long sojourn on death row, the cheering, jeering crowds outside the penitentiary and, inevitably, the traditional hearty breakfast of the condemned man. Usually, it turns out to be something like a double order of Big Macs with fries and a giant Coke.

You could call it a sad reflection on the undeveloped state of the American tastebud that a man should choose kids' stuff like this as his last meal on earth. Then again, perhaps childish food is just the sort of thing that you would want at such a time. Perhaps in this situation I'd want to eat what I remember most fondly from infancy (meat and two veg, I'm afraid: lamb served in very fatty gravy with a very light Yorkshire pudding).

Still, the choice is disappointing. Here, after all, is an opportunity, if ever there was one, to indulge in a bit of fantasy; at the very least you could ask for something that would put your jailers to a lot of trouble and expense. I think I might choose fugu, the Japanese blowfish that, if not properly deveined before it's served, is fatally poisonous. So, with any luck, I could at one stroke satisfy my curiosity and save the executioner a job.

Now, even Lévi-Strauss would have to admit that fugu is civilised, though much of it is served raw. The fugu that reaches the Japanese table very definitely does not belong to nature. Fugu chefs are skilled in removing the poisonous parts of the fish—veins, ovaries, liver—and the specially licensed restaurants in which they work usually serve a complete fugu meal exquisitely presented: fugu fins soaked in hot sake, raw fugu with a sour dipping sauce, a sort of fugu hotpot and a rice porridge made with liquid left over from the hotpot. But even if I did decide to have this as my last meal, I can understand, I think, why someone else might not want it. I doubt whether any of it—even the rice porridge, which by all accounts has quite a rich flavour—can give you the sort of mouthfilling satisfaction that a Big Mac can give.

The point about the Big Mac—or anything that's just been served dripping with grease from the barbie or sizzling from the oven—is that it tastes thoroughly cooked. This is because at some stage in the heating process it underwent the transformation that is now known as the Maillard reaction.

In the early years of this century, Louis-Camille Maillard, a young physician, was investigating proteins. These—the basic elements of much that is vital and active in plant and animal life—are themselves built up out of smaller compounds, the amino acids. Maillard was trying to find out what happens when you heat amino acids together with sugars. What happens, he discovered, is that the solution turns brown and releases aromas character-istic of the particular amino acids you're using. When you roast your coffee beans or malt your barley or barbecue your meat (or fry it, or cook it in the oven), the result is the same: a brown colour and distinctive, complex aromas and flavours. No food in its natural form can afford us sensory experience so intricate: though uncook-ed ripe fruits come close, which suggests to the food writer Harold McGee that our evolutionary ancestors valued cooking with fire, 'in part because it transformed blandness into fruitlike richness'. Venturing further into speculation, McGee also notes that the extremely complex aromas released by cooking with fire are com-pounded of aroma molecules similar to, or identical with, those found in nature: 'In a sip of coffee or a piece of crackling there are echoes of flowers and leaves, fruit and earth, a recapitulation of moments from the long dia-logue between animals and plants.' This, it may be, is why even I, perhaps even a Japanese, might *in extremis* find a Big Mac more comforting than even the most exquisitely prepared piece of raw fugu.

Boiling the fugu wouldn't help, of course, because water boils at a temperature well below that at which the Maillard reaction becomes noticeable. This also is why boiling has always been a less problematic process than roasting, grilling or frying: if you want to try your hand at these, you really need to be something of a lord of the flames. 'There has never been any real reason for a gourmand to cross the channel other than to sample roast or grilled meats,' said the great French gastronome Grimod de La Reynière in the early years of the last century. 'This advantage is owed to the quality of the fuel, for coal produces a more ardent and aggressive heat than wood does, seizing the joint the moment it is put before it, closing the pores, before the meat is cooked, resulting in the concentration of the juices rather than their evaporation.' And he adds that this is all very well for great hunks of beef, but it would char a chicken.

This is, in fact, a rather inaccurate description of what happens when meat is cooked, but the idea of an ardent and aggressive flame is certainly one that would have warmed the heart of a contemporary cook. In the age before gas, the control of heat meant a lot to cooks and, come the middle of the eighteenth century, they turned for help to the new technology of the iron foundry. They tried everything: first the familiar array of spits, roasting pans and chafing dishes; then ovens with an elaborate mechanism of flues running all over the range; then the closed range, in which all the smoke was drawn through flues straight up the chimney so that no heat was lost.

What was going on here was not just an attempt to control the fire and to prevent heat loss, but also to keep smoke out of the food. Earlier cooks, preparing everything over an open wood fire, would have had no chance.

Smoke can be useful, of course. Hold your food sufficiently far from the fire for the heat to dry it but not cook it and you'll have something palatable that will keep during the lean months of winter. However, the diners of past times probably found the taste of smoke far too familiar to be in any way charming. To us—with our Saturday barbecues or the smoke flavouring that we brush over our food if we have neither barbecues nor sense— the taste of burnt wood or charcoal is evocative and comforting. To our ancestors, though they knew nothing of the carcinogens created or released when food is cooked over an open flame, food that tasted of fire probably tasted like death.

# g is for gross

Travellers' tales aren't what they were. We no longer have blank spaces on our maps bearing the legend, 'here be monsters'; we've given up on sea serpents and unicorns and men whose heads do grow beneath their shoulders. But one piece of ignoble savagery haunts the imagination still. We see a monkey led chained into a room by oriental hands. In the centre of the room is a circular table around which sit the diners, wealthy people of refined and exquisite tastes, with their chopsticks and spoons and bowls of rice. In the centre of their circular table is a circular hole, just big enough to accommodate the monkey's head, just small enough to prevent movement. What happens next? Is it a knife they use? A mallet? A trepanning saw? Whatever they do, it is not intended to cause death—this is essential to the story—because the monkey is still alive when they dip their spoons or their chopsticks into its brain and convey the warm portions to their rice bowls.

Should we believe that this happens, or has ever happened? The story turns up in *The Woman Warrior*, Maxine Hong Kingston's account of her life as a Chinese-American in the California of the 1940s and 1950s, but there it has a dream-like, mythic quality. 'Do you know what people in China eat when they have the money?' Maxine Hong Kingston's Chinese mother would say to her children, before telling them over again the fearful tale.

I had long been sceptical of the story when, in 1988, I heard it again from a representative of the World Society for the Protection of Animals. He, however, had evidence, or so he said: the *South China Morning Post* and the Asian Pacific Peoples' Environmental Network.

So I rang the Network in Penang and discovered that it had published a memorandum on the subject. This describes in detail the specially designed table in which the unfortunate monkey is held secure, the upper part of its head protruding through a hole in the top. And it recounts the macabre ritual: the scalpel cutting though the vault of the skull to expose the palpitating brain, which, soaked in brandy, is then scooped out with a spoon or sucked up with a straw. 'Meanwhile,' we're told, 'tears can be seen flowing down the monkey's eyes as its body convulses.'

Unpleasant stuff, and full of circumstantial detail, but when I asked an official of the Network about their source of information I was informed that they'd been told it by a friend. Could they name eye-witnesses? No, the practice is illegal, so people are afraid to admit to it.

But surely there can't be many crimes for which no eye-witnesses at all can ever be found. Remaining sceptical, I turned to the *South China Morning Post*. Here, the evidence turned out to be an interview with a Mr Chen, manager of the Dragon and Phoenix Restaurant in Guangzhou. Mr Chen does indeed own up to serving the brains of dead monkeys, but he claims that the custom of serving them live was banned by the Communists. It may have been, but when I mentioned the matter to Alice Erh Soon Tay, Professor of Jurisprudence at Sydney University, she pointed out to me that people are quite often keen to ingratiate themselves with the present regime by crediting it with putting an end to the barbaric practices of old. Professor Tay, a native of Singapore, has no knowledge of monkey brains ever having been eaten in this way, though, she said, echoing Maxine Hong Kingston, 'we liked that sort of story as children'.

She could not remember when she had first heard the story, but there is at least one person who claims to have been around when it was concocted. It happened in Singapore in March 1952, according to the British food writer Derek Cooper, and it was a practical joke improvised for the benefit of one Arthur Helliwell, a visiting journalist. Arthur worked for the lurid English Sunday paper the *People*, so he was a ready audience for the story his friends told him when he asked them the purpose of the circular hole he'd noticed in the centre of a restaurant table. Not long afterwards, horrified readers of the *People* learned from Helliwell's article much what I was later to learn from the Asian Pacific Peoples' Environmental Network (though he said that monkey brains were supposed to increase virility, while the Network said that they were eaten as an aphrodisiac, which may or may not amount to the same thing).

Of course, there's no doubt that monkeys are eaten. David Melville, of the World Wildlife Fund in Hong Kong, told me that, though monkeys could no longer be bought in the markets of what was then the Crown Colony, they were still available on the mainland. They were sold live, for eating, though he did not know exactly what their purchasers did with them.

He also told me that he had never met anybody who had sat down in a restaurant to a meal of live monkey brains, though he was interested to learn from me about something that had appeared on the front page of the *Asian Wall Street Journal* in 1983. The headline is 'Colony's taste for Exotic Meats Roasts Animal Society' and it's the old story: elaborate Chinese feast, table with hole in the centre, live monkey, shaved head. As usual, there are no eye-witnesses, though the article does quote Fred Thomas, who at the time was Controller of the Hong Kong chapter of the Royal Society for the Prevention of Cruelty to Animals. Thomas, though not an eye-witness, did claim to have proof: four years before, his colleagues had saved a monkey on the run from a restaurant in Kowloon, its head shaved for the table; a year before that, they had found a dead monkey minus its shaved pate and its brains, which had been scooped away.

Well, the dead monkey could have had its brains removed after death. As for the live monkey, the British food writer Paul Levy has pointed out that 'it is always possible that the currency of the story has led some people to imitate art.' Apparently, there are rumours in Hong Kong that somebody once staged a monkey brain feast for a visiting film crew (perhaps for the Italians who made the emetic *Mondo Cane* in 1961). Levy, himself a sceptic, asked a noted Hong Kong gastronome about it. The gastronome asked his aged father: neither of them was shocked by the idea, but neither of them knew anything about the practice. Of course, the Chinese are notoriously omnivorous, though Ken Hom, Chinese-American chef and writer, does in fact think that the idea of eating the brains of live monkeys would be shocking to them: 'we haven't eaten anything raw since the Han Dynasty . . .' he says, 'the Chinese have an aversion to anything raw, let alone something live.' And, he added, you never meet anybody who claims to have done it, only people who've heard about it.

More than anything else, it was the obstinate lack of eye-witnesses that always seemed to give the story its air of urban myth. Like the tales of the vanishing hitch-hiker and the Gucci kangaroo, it was always something that happened to friends of friends. Then I met somebody who said he'd been there.

We were in a large hotel in Sydney at a lunch to celebrate the award of some culinary Oscars and he told me about it over the cheese and coffee. It had happened some twelve years before, he said (which would put it around 1977), when he was visiting a large South-East Asian city on business. Some friends, all of them locals, took him to a restaurant just off a main street in the central business district. They all sat round a circular table in the centre of which a hole had been cut. The maitre d' rapped on the table and a monkey's head appeared, protruding through the hole about fifteen or twenty centimetres. What sort of monkey? My friend didn't know. Then the maitre d' produced a knife and sliced off the top of the monkey's head; with one blow, apparently, though a certain amount of trimming was necessary to reveal the brain.

'How does the monkey react to all this?' I asked.

'Not very well at all,' replied my friend. In fact, he told me, he hadn't reacted too well himself: with a mixture of moral and physical revulsion, he'd left and returned to his hotel.

Had he seen spirits poured into the monkey's exposed brain? No, but there were spirit bottles on the table, which might have been used for that purpose after he'd gone.

Did his companions, all of them Asian, regard these proceedings as being in any way unusual? No, they looked upon it as a treat, a special occasion, but not as a once-in-a-lifetime thing.

He told me all this readily enough, but only on the understanding that I wouldn't use his name without the agreement of his Asian employers. It was the same outfit that he and his companions had been working for on the night of the monkey brain feast, so I wasn't altogether surprised to learn a few days later that this sort of thing was not on the whole regarded by them as good PR. I hope I've kept faith with my informant: I haven't told you who he was, who he worked for or where it is all supposed to have happened.

So now you, reader, are probably in the position that I used to be in: you haven't heard it from an eye-witness, but you have heard about it from somebody who claims to have heard about it from someone who actually saw it. This is hearsay evidence, and you are quite at liberty to decide that it is not acceptable. If you do decide not to accept it, you may still be wondering about the hole in the centre of the table. Nobody questions the reality of the hole: it's used for *ke-tze*, or steamboat, and it holds the dish which contains the broth, heated from beneath by a charcoal fire, in which the meat and vegetables are cooked. You do this yourself in the steamboat, so they're all very freshly cooked. Fresh but not raw, of course.

# h is for Hawaii

On a beach in Hawaii I tasted what was easily one of the sweetest things I have ever eaten. It was a piece of dried pineapple and its sweetness was so pure, so free of acidity, so uncloying, that I felt I could have gone on eating it forever, even though I seldom greatly enjoy sweet things. It was the produce of a very friendly man who had been in Hawaii for just nine years, having spent most of his working life as an employee of Northwestern Bell Telephones in Minneapolis.

Of course, what with the cool of the tropical evening and the unfamiliar pleasures of sweetness, I wasn't in the mood for political questions. Why should I have been? The Hawaiian experience is the product of two centuries of political tragedy, but my experience of Hawaii (product of two days there) had been of the kind that does not encourage political interrogation. It was the usual tourist gig: I stepped off the plane, caressed by soft, warm air and greeted by routine '*alohas*', and was duly garlanded with a cheap *lei* formed of wilting blooms strung on wire. You know, or you suspect, that this sort of thing isn't for real—that it panders to expectations created less by a study of the great Hawaiian creation chant *Kumulipo* than by an old Elvis movie—but at the time it's difficult to care.

I'm home now, though, primed with histories of the islands and with a scepticism born of talking with one or two indigenous Hawaiians, and I'm ready to ask some political questions about what I ate on the beach.

So, why pineapple and why a man from Minneapolis?

Pineapple is very big in the Hawaiian archipelago and has been for a long time, though it has always played second fiddle to sugar. 'King Sugar and his son Pineapple', somebody once called them: plantation crops both, occupying many hectares, feeding an international hunger for sweet things.

In 1778, Captain James Cook noted the size and quality of the sugar that he found growing on all the islands, and by the 1830s serious attempts were being made to turn a profit from this luxuriant growth. Though some of the crop was exported to Australia, it was clear that the United States was the most appropriate destination for Hawaiian sugar, and here problems arose: not only was the U.S. market already crowded with imports from countries whose sugar was cheaper than Hawaii's, but it was also protected by high tariffs. Only in 1875 did the plantation owners find a way round the barrier.

In February of that year, the King of Hawaii arrived home from a visit to the United States—he had been received by President Ulysses S. Grant and greeted at Barnum's circus by a band playing 'King of the Cannibal Isles'—with news of a treaty: Hawaiian sugar would be allowed into the United States free of tariffs in exchange for a promise that no Hawaiian territory would be ceded to foreign powers (which meant that though the U.S. wasn't getting Pearl Harbor, nobody else would get it either).

But sixteen years later, the United States removed the tariff on imports of raw sugar, protecting its domestic industry with a bounty paid to the growers. This was devastating news for the plantation owners, who now had to compete for the American market on equal terms with the rest of the world and on unequal terms with the domestic American industry. Wouldn't it be better, then, if Hawaiian sugar was no longer foreign? Wouldn't it be better if Hawaii were to be annexed by the United States?

Perhaps it would be better for the people too. 'It will be better for the colored man to have the white man rule,' wrote one planter. 'It is better for the colored man of India and Australia that the white man rules, and it is better here that the white man should rule ...' Economically speaking, the white man did rule, since it was he who owned the plantations that provided Hawaii with what was almost its only means of economic support. The plantation owners were the richest people in the kingdom, and accordingly paid the highest rates of tax, but they were foreigners and could have only an indirect influence on the government. Of course, these men were not by nature revolutionaries, but they formed a club in which to discuss the opportunities for reform. It was called the Annexation Club.

Attempts by the indigenous monarchy to reassert its power were unavailing; by the will of its most powerful citizens, Hawaii became a territory of the United States in 1898. The native Hawaiians were not dispossessed by armies or battle ships. The dispossession of 1898 happened without violence, and that was because a more grave dispossession, a mental dispossession, had already occurred. This too had to do with food.

When Captain Cook first came to the islands there were about a million people living there, labouring on the land together, supported solely by their own produce. It was just as well that food was so abundant: the British consumed it so avidly as to cause the Hawaiians to fear that—like aliens in a 1950s science fiction movie who invade the earth from a dying planet—they had come to Hawaii because there was nothing left to eat in their own country. Perhaps they had come to eat the people too: there is evidence that the British and the Hawaiians each suspected the other of cannibalism.

Of course, nobody was eaten—not even Captain Cook,

who was killed and, as a mark of respect, dismembered and roasted—but the moment that British ships dropped anchor in the archipelago, something began to eat at the Hawaiian spirit. Naturally, there was physical disease, the usual stowaway when European ships made for another hemisphere, and, as always, a very efficient agent of imperialism. A hundred years later, the indigenous population had been so wasted by illness that the sugar growers had to import labour from overseas to work the plantations. But it was not just a sickness of the body that troubled the Hawaiians. Those of them who did manage to make it to the cane fields did not impress their employers; they were widely believed to be lazy, unambitious and apathetic. Something had happened, something was gone. They had lost their traditional system of beliefs and it had happened, quite suddenly, one day in 1819.

Until then, Hawaiian chiefs had kept their subjects in awe by a system of taboos called 'kapus'. Everything in Hawaiian life—politics, religion, agriculture, sex, food and play—was governed by kapus. 'It was a fixed principle, always there, just as shadow was an inevitable part of a sunlit day,' writes the Australian historian Gavan Daws. 'To step into the shadow to violate the kapus, even accidentally, was to forfeit the right to live.'

The kapus were doomed from the moment Europeans arrived in Hawaii. 'The ladies are very lavish of their favours ...' said one of Cook's men, who seems not to have approved of this sort of thing, though his shipmates were on the whole more enthusiastic. In Hawaiian terms there was nothing wrong with what the women were doing—it was wise to give generously, even of your own body, to such powerful beings—but once on board ship, they were tempted to do something that was very wrong in Hawaiian terms: they ate with the men.

In Hawaii, men dined with the gods and women were never invited; their food couldn't even be cooked in the same ovens as the men's. But on British ships, the women not only got to eat with the men, they also allowed themselves to eat food that was normally forbidden them, like pork, bananas and coconuts. They knew that to do so was to break a kapu, but they knew as well that their bodies gave them more power among the white men than they enjoyed in their own society. As more and more foreign ships visited the islands, the kapus were more frequently broken, and, of course, nothing happened. Some of the transgressors paid with their lives but the skies did not fall.

So, by the early nineteenth century, the way had been made ready for the woman whose desire for political power was to destroy the kapu system: Kaahumanu, favourite among the twenty-one wives of King Kamehameha. She was an enthusiastic violator of kapus—as early as 1810, she had broken the kapus on the eating of pork and of shark's meat by women—and in 1819, when her husband died, she announced her intention of breaking free of the old ways: 'We intend that the husband's food

75

and the wife's food shall be cooked in the same oven, and that they shall eat out of the same calabash. We intend to eat pork and bananas and coconuts, and to live as the white people do.'

Not six months after the old chief's death, Kaahumanu suggested to his successor, Liholiho, that he join her, his mother and some other women at a meal on the Big Island, not far from where I tasted the pineapple. He knew what this meant, of course, and, facing the prospect with due seriousness, spent a couple of days on a boat out at sea, awash with indecision and drunkenness. At length he came ashore and invited all the leading chiefs and several foreigners to a feast. There were two tables, one for men and one for women, both set in the European style. Everybody else was already eating when the king—drunk, as some accounts have it—wandered around the tables, then suddenly sat down with the women and began to eat. He ate voraciously, according to report, 'but was evidently much perturbed'. The guests were astonished; they clapped their hands and cried, '*Ai noa*—the eating tabu is broken.'

From that moment, the old gods were finished; by royal order, their idols were burnt and their temples were torn down. The psychic rug had been pulled from under the feet of the native Hawaiians. Some continued to follow the ancient ways in secret, but the rest were very open to the blandishments of the first boatload of Christian missionaries, who arrived the following year.

So food has shaped the destiny of Hawaii in more ways than one. The charming man from Minneapolis was part of a plantation culture which the old Hawaiians would have thought very strange: you turn your productive land over to food crops, which you export in order to make money so that you can buy the food that you need to eat and which you can't grow yourself because you no longer have enough land left on which to grow it. The old Hawaiians, in the days before sugar and pineapple ruled their destiny, lived under what the anthropologist Marshall Sahlins calls 'an economy of determinate ends and sufficient means': the main product of the islands was food; the main food was the starchy root taro—'*kaolo*' to the Hawaiians, who held it in such high regard that it played an important role in their creation myth—which was eaten steamed or pounded into the paste known as '*poi*'. Not even dry poi can be stored for more than six weeks so there was no possibility of amassing a great surplus of the stuff. The Hawaiians were skilful cultivators, but there was no point in producing more taro than was necessary to meet their immediate needs and those of their chiefs. To Europeans and Americans, accustomed to turning surplus into profit, this looked like sheer idleness. No wonder they thought the land and its inhabitants better off under their governance.

Dispossessed of their lands, betrayed by their gods, racked by disease, the native beneficiaries of the plantations owners' economic reforms reacted as people often do whose self-esteem is low: they ate the wrong sort of food and they ate lots of it. Today, rates of death from heart disease and stroke among the indigenous people of Hawaii are more than three times the U.S. national average, and the rate of deaths from diabetes is nearly seven times the national average.

Yet there's ample evidence that traditional Hawaiian life was very healthy, even though myth has clouded our vision of what it was like. Ask yourself what mental image you have of native Hawaiians. Rotund, perhaps? Fat, even? A day or two after my encounter with the pineapple, I met Dr Terry Shintani of the Wai'anae Comprehensive Health Center on the island of Oahu. He agreed that this has long been the prevailing stereotype. 'Many people think that Hawaiians are naturally a very obese people,' he told me. 'One study has shown that prevalence of obesity among native Hawaiians is about 66 per cent. It's among the highest in the United States.' This, in such an overweight country, is not a statistic to be proud of. Yet old pictures and the reports of the earliest European visitors to the islands tell a different story. The reports speak of a people who are 'well formed, with fine muscular limbs', who 'walk very gracefully, run nimbly and are capable of bearing great fatigue', and pictures from well into the age of photography bear out these claims. (It's true that Hawaiian chiefs were traditionally men of great bulk, but they would not have stood out so impressively if their people had not been a good deal smaller than they.)

Dr Shintani thinks that much of the change has to do with food. The traditional Hawaiian diet was high in complex carbohydrates and low in fat: taro, breadfruit, sweet potato, lots of green vegetables, fruit, a little fish, with seaweed as a salty condiment and an excellent source of calcium. Today, native Hawaiians eat what the rest of the population eats: a diet high in calories, fats, sugar and animal products. I suppose there must have been a transitional stage between these two diets; perhaps we can glimpse it in an interview recorded in 1977 with a women called Eleanor Harvey, born in 1912 of a Hawaiian-Chinese mother and an Australian father:

> My mother was typical Hawaiian. It was either raw fish, poi or dried fish. If it was stew meat, you won't find potatoes, you won't find onions in there, you won't find no vegetables, 'cause Mama only wanted her meat with gravy. That's all. That's it. No more potatoes, no more nothing. She said she didn't want all the junks inside.

Dr Shintani decided to increase the junks inside some of his patients. He placed twenty of them, all indigenous Hawaiians, on a traditional diet for three weeks. They could eat as much as they wanted, providing that they chose only the traditional foods of their culture. The results, according to Dr Shintani, were spectacular. There was an average weight loss of between five and nearly eight kilos; some lost as much as thirteen kilos. Their cholesterol levels fell by 12–14 per cent and—more impressive than any of this—their diabetes responded very quickly to the change of diet.

The indigenous Hawaiian population is no longer very large, but what if they all wanted to eat traditional foods? Would there be enough taro to go round? 'At this point, there would not be,' said Dr Shintani. 'Today there is very little taro production. It's very expensive. But we want to exert some pressure on the agricultural community to make it available for these purposes, because, of course, we have demonstrated the healthful effects on many diseases of this traditional diet.'

But there are signs of change. The plantation crops no longer pay as well as they used to and some of the land on which they once grew is now being returned to local produce. It isn't much but it's a beginning; not, perhaps, the beginning of a return to indigenous foodways, but at least the beginning of the end of plantation culture.

This is a cautionary tale, or rather it would be if there was anybody left who could benefit from the caution it teaches.

# i is for ink

One of my favourite recipes is for a dish called The Feast of the Three Fishermen of Calafell. For it, you need two kilos of fish, one each of octopus, tomatoes and rice, four kilos of potatoes, half a kilo of onions, four heads of garlic, four dried hot chilli peppers and a slice of bread. The recipe, which was set down by Irving Davis in 1969, begins as follows:

'First of all take a plane to Barcelona, then drive to Calafell, then find your fishermen and go with them about four o'clock to Villanova and get them to choose the fish as it is landed.' How it continues is hardly important, because you're not going to Barcelona, are you? And even if you were, you probably wouldn't be going to Calafell; and if you were to go there, you'd probably find that thirty years of tourism and pollution have altered the culinary picture somewhat for fisherfolk in those parts.

I can't speak with certainty about it myself, because I haven't been to Calafell, and this recipe, which I haven't tried, is one of my favourites only because of the way it confounds our expectations of what a recipe should be. We expect a recipe to be useful, we expect it to tell us how to do things, but this isn't a useful recipe at all; it's simply the record of how a certain group of people living at a particular place did things at a particular time. (Actually, there are more recipes like this than we usually admit: a lot of books by chefs are simply records of what goes on in a particular restaurant, written with lofty disdain for the needs of the home cook.)

Patience Gray, who quotes this recipe in her book *Honey From a Weed*, does so, I presume, because it perfectly embodies her belief that food is inseparable from the land, from the seasons, from the life of the people. She's right, of course, and out of her conviction produced a beautiful book, but I for one find that I can take only so much of this sort of thing: this Norman Douglas world of stones and earthenware pots, white-washed walls and red-tiled roofs, gnarled old peasants full of ancient wisdom and strange whimsy, inefficient plumbing, traditional misogyny, painful births and early deaths. I'm not likely to go there, and if I were I'd probably have to contend with the traffic coming in the opposite direction: young people in search of decent wages and urban pleasures. There might be other traffic, too, trucking the local produce along the narrow roads to the delicatessens and restaurants of the world. There ought to be a way of writing about food that, free alike from *nostalgie de la boue* and urban smugness, does justice to all this traffic.

It doesn't seem much to ask that food writers should care about where the food has come from and where it is going. It doesn't seem much, but it's a pretty rare thing to find. Your average large, slim, glossy cookery book may show you pictures of farms, fieldworkers and so on, but it has about as much interest in the realities of food production as Marie Antoinette had when she put on a bonnet and made like a shepherdess.

A teacher of food technology once told me that she sometimes gets her students to try out recipes from large, glossy cookery books. It turns out that a lot of them just don't work and can't be made to work, a fact which often goes unnoticed because there's usually little to interrupt your average cookery book in its progress from publisher's warehouse to remaindered bookshop. Quite a few of these books do get bought, of course, and I suppose there must be a handful of purchasers who, having laid out their $29.95, will want their money's worth. They'll try out a recipe or two. So will all those people who've been given the book by someone who expects to see gratitude embodied in a steaming plate of something exotically beautiful that looks just like the picture on page 87. If the recipe doesn't work, they'll attribute failure to their own incompetence or to the fact that they had to omit the lemon juice because the local supermarket had run out of little yellow plastic containers of the stuff.

None of this matters very much, because there are already enough recipes in the world and what most people really need is not another cookery book but a book that tells them about ingredients and seasonality. There are such books, of course, but even they often contain recipes, because recipes—morbidly precise as to quantities and times, assuming no knowledge of what is being cooked or of the process by which it is cooked—are what we have come to expect.

These expectations have been growing steadily in extent and confidence since the fifteenth century, and for a good reason, too, though that reason is sometimes overlooked. When Anne Willan, a writer normally sensitive to processes of historical change, tells us that the renaissance cook Martino was the first 'to give detailed cooking instructions and tips that show he is thoroughly at home with his recipes,' it's difficult not to suspect that she has forgotten the most important technological innovation to occur in Martino's lifetime. His tips and detailed instructions may reveal a new familiarity with the processes of cooking, but it's equally probable that they imply something else: the presence of a readership ignorant enough to need detailed instruction and the availability of a new means of meeting their needs. By contrast, Taillevent, the renowned fourteenth-century cook whose recipes Willan describes as 'little more than lists of ingredients strung together with a few instructions', was a pro

writing for fellow pros; but what most separates his man-
uscript from Martino's book is the fact that the latter was,
as Willan tells us, 'printed in Rome in 1474'. Brought to
the world by means of the latest technology, Martino's
recipes were a portent of what was to come.

It's not always obvious who the first printed cookery
books were aimed at. 'What was the point,' as one historian asks, 'of publishing vernacular manuals outlining
procedures that were already familiar to all skilled
practitioners of certain crafts?' In the case of Martino's
recipes, though, it's fairly clear what the point was. They
turn up in a book called *De Honesta Voluptate et Valetudine*,
written by one Bartolomeo Platina, a librarian at the
Vatican. Platina wrote in Latin for scholarly readers whom
it is difficult to imagine breaking off from a hard day's
work at the coalface of renaissance humanism—all those
epistles in the style of Horace, orations on the dignity of
man and arse-licking letters to potential royal patrons—
in order to rustle up some risotto or stuff a crayfish. It's
unlikely, though not impossible, that they bought the
book for the recipes. Presumably they, like the author,
had broader prospects in view. As his title indicated,
Platina was offering them instruction on 'honest enjoyment and good health', and recipes were just a part of
his scheme: he also had advice to impart about diet, nutrition and table manners, a combination of topics that
to this day recurs in cookery book after cookery book.

In the following century books like this, books that

claimed to tell you how to do things—how to live healthily, how to live virtuously, how to rule a kingdom or sing madrigals, how to draw, bake clay, build bridges—poured forth from the presses in a steady stream. Printers (who were the publishers of the day) had a living to earn; obviously it was in their interests both to foster and to satisfy a new lust for self-improvement, self-education and independence. Unfortunately, it's doubtful whether a book will by itself make you a skilful and independent operator in the kitchen, and the philosopher Michael Oakeshott has memorably expressed these doubts with clarity and stiff elegance:

> It might be supposed that an ignorant man, some edible materials, and a cookery book compose together the necessities of a self-moved (or concrete) activity called cooking. But nothing is further from the truth. The cookery book is not an independently generated beginning from which cooking can spring; it is nothing more than an abstract of somebody's knowledge of how to cook: it is the stepchild, not the parent of the activity. The book, in its turn, may help to set a man on to dressing a dinner, but if it were his sole guide he could never, in fact, begin: the book speaks only to those who know already the kind of thing to expect from it and consequently how to interpret it.

This might seem to imply simply that you can't cook a dish yourself until somebody else has cooked it for you, and this probably wouldn't have embarrassed Platina's readers, who all, no doubt, employed their own cooks. But Oakeshott's remarks arise from considerations deeper than this. He observes that the skilled practitioners of any art—whether it's cookery, drawing or ruling a kingdom—all possess a kind of knowledge that cannot be written down. This is practical knowledge, the feel of the craft, the kind of knowledge that, says Oakeshott, 'can be acquired only by continuous contact with one who is perpetually practising it'.

Cajun cooking provides a good example of the sort of thing Oakeshott seems to have in mind. Much of it is based on a roux made by mixing flour with oil and cooking them together until they brown. The exact degree of brownness required will vary depending on the dish being cooked, but gumbo demands a deep brown roux. As far as I can tell, this means cooking the flour until just before it burns. I suppose you could get some idea of how to do this by burning a few roux, but it would be better to learn by watching somebody who knows how to do it.

Perhaps the terseness of Taillevent's recipes derives from a belief that it's useless to set down recipes for people who don't already know what to do with them. Martino's, or Platina's, tips and detailed instructions— written for people who presumably were not in continuous contact with their cooks—are an early attempt to bridge the gap between what can and cannot be written down.

More than five hundred years later, this gap is as wide as ever it was, though our attempts to bridge it have become more sophisticated: books full of pictures that take you step-by-step through the cooking process, videos, CD-ROMs. They can't do it, of course—the gap is unbridgeable—but they can do something else, and that something is very regrettable: they can fill you with the desire to cook things. They can suggest to you a dish that you might like to cook and then leave you to buy the ingredients and put them together. This is an inversion of what used to be the order of things. To quote Oakeshott again, 'A cook is not a man who first has a vision of a pie and then tries to make it; he is a man skilled in cookery, and both his projects and his achievements spring from that skill.' This is the correct order.

After all, what do cooks do and how do they do it? Cooks are people who take what is edible from their environment and make it palatable. They may do this by arranging it or cutting it up or heating it, or any two of these things or all three of them. The environment may be natural, demanding a knowledge of seasons and landscape; it may be agricultural, demanding a knowledge of cultivation; or it may be urban, demanding a knowledge of markets, shops and prices. The environment may be rich in food or poor in it; in either case, the cook has to be able to turn circumstance to advantage, to improvise with what is available.

This is subtle, creative work and the most grateful

diners have always acknowledged the skill of the best cooks: 'O ye immortal Gods,' cried Platina, 'which cook could compete with my friend Martino of Como ...' The outburst comes at the end of a recipe for *biancomangiare*, a dish whose preparation is very long and tedious; just the sort of thing that you might be happy to know about but which you would prefer to leave to the professionals.

Cooking *biancomangiare* was no fun, but why should it have been? Whoever the earliest printed cookery books were intended for—the professional cook, the professional cook's employer, the interested observer—there was never any reason for them to pretend that they were offering a good time to anyone apart from the lucky few who'd actually get to eat the food.

Cooking started to be fun when the middle classes began doing it for themselves. No doubt the humble cooks of old, preparing meals for their own families or for the families they served, sometimes derived deep satisfaction and pleasure from their work, but nobody ever suggested that it was something you'd do if you didn't have to. Things had to change when a dearth of domestic servants forced people with money to start fending for themselves. Cooking now had to be fun and creative, because, if it wasn't fun and creative, why were People Like Us doing it?

Before that time, cookery books (genuine cookery books, not lifestyle manuals like Platina's) were at the stage computer manuals are at now. At best, computer

manuals are taut, practical volumes; these days many of
them look friendly and approachable, but even the cheer-
iest of them give the distinct impression that their cheer-
iness is a sugar-coating for the bitter didactic pill. If
there's an Elizabeth David of the computer world, I've yet
to come across her.

The very first Australian cookery book, Edward
Abbott's *English and Australian Cookery Book*, published in
1864, is a good example of a user-friendly computer
manual of the kitchen. It has all sorts of general advice
to offer, some of it priggish ('Remember, in partaking of
a luxuriant meal, how many in the world there are who
would be glad of the crumbs'), some of it still relevant
('If you employ tradesmen in building double the esti-
mate'). The tone is always chirpy, but it's the chirpiness
of the schoolteacher who wants to get on well with the
class.

The admonitory tone of Victorian cookbooks like
Abbott's survived well into this century. 'Many a good
cook's reputation has been built on the ability to make
an omelette': the advice—and it's very good advice—
comes from *The Margaret Fulton Cookbook*, published in
1968, but it could have come from Edward Abbott or
Isabella Beeton or any number of books of household
management written for anxious nineteenth-century new-
lyweds. The Margaret Fulton of a quarter-century ago
follows the Victorian model even in her fear that her
readers might be tempted to overstep the mark. On the

subject of hors d'oeuvres she warns that, 'Attempting too many varieties has been the downfall of many a hostess and death to the meal that follows.'

The 'hostess'—ever anxious to get things right and fearful that the next canapé may prove her downfall—is no longer Margaret Fulton's presumed reader, but Stephanie Alexander's book, *Stephanie's Seasons*, published in 1993, is a measure of how far we've come, and the appearance of the Los Angeles riots in its pages is probably some sort of first for culinary writing. Previously, the most violent reference you were likely to come across in a cookery book would be to some ancient passage of arms, like Pavia or Marengo, that had given its name to a dish and was sufficiently distant in time and space to seem picturesque. Here, though, the riots are present as the very immediate context in which some of the cooking has to get done. 'People are dying,' writes Stephanie Alexander. 'The violence is unspeakable. By nightfall it was reported that there were three hundred fires burning in Los Angeles. There was a sense of unreality in the kitchen.'

I bet there was, but how much reality of this sort do we want in our cookbooks? *Stephanie's Seasons* is a diary of the culinary year: the year in question was 1992 and Stephanie Alexander was a guest chef in Los Angeles during April of that year, so the riots could hardly be left out, but why a diary in the first place? Because food writing has long since ceased to be a matter purely of recipes, or even of 'honest enjoyment and good health'. It is a vehicle of entertainment for the reader and of self-expression for the writer. Pleasures which in the past were incidental—the little personal touches that enliven the sober prose of an Edward Abbott or an Isabella Beeton—are fast becoming the central point of the whole enterprise. They're no longer the sugar that coats the pill; they are sweet little confections in their own right.

But passing centuries and changing fashions have not altered the question that all food writers have to ask themselves: how much to put in? It is, of course, a question facing any writer who aspires to instruct. Take, for example, the book of instructions that came with your video recorder. Often translated from the Japanese by somebody who learned English in Osaka by reading the subtitles on old episodes of *Star Trek*, these flimsy volumes combine maximum comprehensiveness with minimum clarity.

The temptation to try to get it all in has always been there: in the last century, they tried to tell you everything about running a household; in the 1950s, they tried to tell you everything about holding a dinner party. Nowadays, the temptation is slightly different. We don't need cookery books any more than we need *Star Trek*—we can go out, or order in, or bung something in the microwave—so the cookery book has evolved. (If other literary genres were as skilled at adapting to survive, we'd still be reading epic poems and blank verse tragedies.) The modern cookery book tempts you with meltingly beautiful pictures and prose that tells of exotic or sophisticated delights. Then it gives you recipes, and since everything is so terribly sophisticated or so bloody exotic, the recipes have to be very, very comprehensive. This is the sort of writing against which Patience Gray was making a stand when she quoted the recipe for The Feast of the Three Fishermen of Calafell.

I wish I could say that I've learnt from her example. I wish I could say that I have acted on my own advice and apprenticed myself to a real cook so that I could acquire the sort of skill that can be acquired only by continuous contact with one who is perpetually practising it. But I haven't: I collect large, slim, glossy cookery books and go out shopping for the ingredients they demand, and when I try to cook a roux I burn it.

# J is for Japan

'Is this Paris?' I asked him.

It certainly looked like Paris. We seemed to be standing in the rain outside the Collège de France in the rue des Ecoles. Over his shoulder I saw a laundry truck nosing its way through the traffic and then breaking free to hurtle too fast along the glistening street.

'Essentially, yes,' said the sad-faced man.

I had heard that Parisian intellectuals tended to be sententious, so I was hoping for just a little dogmatism on the question of where we were. But then perhaps this wasn't Paris and perhaps he was only essentially a Parisian intellectual.

And yet, as I looked down, I saw that same sad face reflected up at me from the back cover of a slim paperback. Nervously, I rang my finger along the spine, along the letters that spelt out, I knew, the name of his book.

*Empire of Signs*, they said. It was his book—no doubt about it—and it contained his Japan, which both delighted and annoyed me; for his Japan was not my Japan, and neither, I suspected, was it the Japanese Japan. This was merely somewhere else of the same name.

'Do you know about Jason and the Argonauts?' he asked, smiling.

'Yup—seen the movie on late-night TV.'

'Then you will know that in the course of their long voyage on the ship *Argo*, the Argonauts carried out so many running repairs on their vessel that they gradually replaced each piece of it. By the end they had a new ship, but they still called it the *Argo*. Was it the *Argo*? The form had not changed, the name had not changed. Only the substance was totally different, but substance, as the Catholics will tell you, is not essence. So, no, where we are is not materially equivalent to what you call Paris, but it is essentially Paris, because Paris is not a collection of stones and people—it is a collection of relations. So is Sydney, so is London, so is New York. So are you.'

'And so—' I began, but changed my mind. 'You know what I want to talk about, don't you?' I tried instead.

'I know everything that you want me to know. After all, it's your—'

'Good. So what about Japan?'

'Japan, for me, is a few features that I have taken from somewhere far away and put together into a system for

95

my book. It is, perhaps, a toy country like your Lilliput. That is what I have chosen to call "Japan".'

'Look,' I said, in a rather vulgar outburst that I soon regretted even at the time, 'the days are gone when Parisian intellectuals were allowed to believe that the world didn't exist except inside their heads. But let me tell you, there is a country called Japan, peopled with real people, living real lives and living them for their own sake, not just to provide you with an elegant intellectual toy to play with.'

I think it was this little speech, more than anything, that made him realise the calibre of person he was dealing with. He wasn't dealing with one of those pallid intellectual groupies who faithfully wrote down his every word. He wasn't dealing with some idle boulevard philosopher, gurgling with glee at each new cerebral *bibelot*. No, he was dealing with a cast of mind that he, in the remote, abstract playpen that he called a life, seldom came across. He was dealing with a real idiot.

'I am not an imperialist,' he said (a little testily, I thought). 'I am not trying to convert another people to Christianity or to liberal democracy, or to hamburgers and Coca-Cola. Nor, incidentally, am I writing a guide book, which is what you seem to think I should be doing. As it happens, I'm as uninterested in the East as the East is in me. All I have taken from it is a few features which I can play with, as one might play with a set of building blocks, constructing out of them a symbolic system entirely unlike our own.'

'So what you want,' I said, 'is a country of the mind—a fictional world that exists only as a contrast to the real one. Previous generations have sought such a country in antiquity, in Greece and Rome. A generation younger than yours finds it in the interstices of a computer's brain.'

'But a system is interesting precisely in the degree to which it is not open to the mere tourist. The Latin grammar, the computer manual, the Japanese dictionary, stand between us and the country we wish to visit, at once beckoning and forbidding.'

Now we were in a restaurant. It was a very discreet restaurant, and Paris, or the essential Paris, was visible only as a triangle of grey sky framed by heavy swags of velvet curtain. At a table opposite us, a short, squat man in a heavy grey suit was talking softly to a much younger woman. She sat demurely, uncertainly, as though conscious of possessing great reserves of power which she was not yet ready to use.

The bill arrived at their table and his conversation, though still whispered, became more urgent, as though he had business that he had delayed until now, but which had to be got through before his little gold piece of plastic was returned to him with its pen and paper.

He grew louder, exasperated. At last he took out his own pen and scribbled urgently on a notepad he had drawn from his top breast pocket. He spoke, audibly now, of street names, numbers, landmarks, and his pen swept across the paper in broad, artistic gestures.

For a little while, my friend and I sat in silence, watching this pantomime. Then he turned back to me.

'She understands every word he speaks,' he said. 'Yet his meaning is as opaque to her as if he were speaking Japanese.'

'I think she knows what he wants,' I said.

'Yes, but there is a banality in her willed misprision. In Japan, on the other hand, one is in a world saturated in signs. The streets have no names—you cannot make an appointment without a map.'

'Yes, I know all about this, and I know about having to recognise restaurants by the characters painted on the curtain placed at their doors, or by their signs, the drawing of a pig for a *tonkatsu* restaurant, the small red lantern for a *yakitori* establishment, or the plastic models they have in their windows of the sort of food they serve.'

'Yes, but how do you get there? Somebody must tell you and, in telling you, must transform his body to a sign, make the body itself known in gesture and drawings.'

The couple departed briskly, in ominous silence, and our first courses arrived: for him, oysters; for me, a duck sausage with *pâté de foie gras*, which he looked at with distrust.

'The oyster,' he said, raising one to his lips, 'has suffered from nothing but the knife that was used to open it. Like Japanese food, where the only operation in the kitchen is that of cutting up.'

'What about sushi?'

'What *about* sushi?'

'Well, you could argue that *nori-maki*—which is the form of sushi that consists of rice, wasabi and seafood rolled together in a flat square of seaweed—is in fact a sort of raw sausage.'

'You could,' he said. 'If you were desperate to prove a point,' he added.

'OK, but what about *tonkatsu*? You take thin slices of pork, season them with salt and pepper, dredge them in flour, coat them in breadcrumbs and deep-fry them. You need a good deal more than a knife to do that.'

Above a bed of salt, his last oyster hung, trembling a little, from his tiny fork. He put it straight into his mouth.

'This is an interesting case,' he said. 'Not unlike *tempura*. In both of them, foreign methods have been adapted to Japanese tastes. "*Ton*" means "pig", and "*katsu*" is a Japanese attempt at "cutlet". It's a very recent dish, too, credited to a chef in Tokyo in 1932. *Tempura*, of course, is not so recent, but its name too betrays its origins. The Japanese in the sixteenth century saw Portuguese soldiers eating deep-fried fish in Lent—"*tempera*", as they called it—and they took up the practice themselves. But the point about *tempura* is not that it is foreign food but that it is foreign food made thoroughly Japanese.'

The empty shells on his plate rattled together as he pushed them away from him.

'France,' he said, 'is the land of the *pomme frite*.' A

waiter passed by us, carrying a small white bowl of bright golden slivers. 'But the fat in which we cook the French fry adds to its heaviness, rather than takes from it.'

'Yes, I know all about this, too. The Japanese take the fried food of the Portuguese and transform it utterly. They have a lumpy batter, made with ice-cold water that just thinly coats the food, and far more oil than most Western cooks use—'

'But with a result that is not oily. Instead, something one never associates with fried food in the West: freshness.'

'Yes, but a good deal more than just cutting up has gone on here.'

'Not really. Ah, thank you.' These last words were addressed to the waiter, who had arrived with roast lamb for my friend and a stewed pig's head for me. 'Not at all, really,' he continued. 'For what does the *tempura* chef do? With a graceful, precise movement of the chopsticks (which we can see, because everything is done in front of us), he conveys the food to the cold, watery batter and from there to the hot oil. He does nothing to it while it is in the oil: it just floats there, or swims, propelled by the evaporation of the water in its coating of batter. Then it emerges like a crystalline form of itself, like those casts at Pompeii, where the solidified lava—shaped like an old man, a girl, a dog, anyone who couldn't get away in time—holds within itself the shape of a body that has long since rotted away. This is neatly emblematic of the whole of Japanese cuisine. It has no heart, no centre. There is no sense of one thing being fundamental to the dish and of other things serving an ornamental function. In Japan, everything ornaments everything else. Nothing is fundamental.'

I was wondering how much of this sort of brilliance it might be polite to listen to before protesting when he interrupted himself.

'There is no sauce,' he said, 'no blending, no enveloping in a crust, none of what we call cookery.'

'But the *tonkatsu* that you're so fond of is always served with sauce. In fact, *tonkatsu* restaurants are very particular about their sauces, and very secretive, too.'

'Pah!' he said, Frenchly. 'What are these secret sauces? Soy, sake, Worcestershire sauce: all of them liquids—'

'There's mustard too. That's not a liquid.'

'It is a paste, which imparts its thickness to the liquids with which it is mixed (or, if you prefer, is itself made more fluid by the liquids that are added to it). But these thickenings and weakenings have nothing in common with the elaborate, alchemical transformations of the European kitchen. Rawness is the essential spirit of Japanese food.'

'Aren't the Japanese supposed to be highly civilised? And aren't you people supposed to be keen on the idea that cooking is what marks civilisation off from savagery?'

He did me his disappointed look, which I wish I could convey adequately: his large, soft eyes didn't flicker,

didn't for a moment lose their expression of benign interest in me, and disappointment was signified only by the
slightest, most eloquent, turning down of the mouth.

'To us,' he said, slowly and patiently, 'rawness reveals
the inner nature of the food. To us, rawness is a matter
of blood and, consequently, of strength and death. But
in Japan, rawness is a purely visual matter—it has nothing
to do with the inner nature of what we eat, because what
we eat has, as I have told you, no heart, no centre. In
Japan, a tray is set before you: boxes, bowls, saucers, little
piles and shreds of food. Nothing is predetermined; your
eating has the freedom of play. You pick some vegetables
here, some rice there; you take a mouthful of soup or of
sake. And, as I said, all that has happened to the food is
that it has been cut up. This has nothing in common with
Western food. *We* are presented with a finished dish, an
elaborate composition put together behind the closed
door of the kitchen, varnished like a painting, embalmed
like a body. We have no choice, or only one: to eat or
not to eat.'

I considered the choices before me. I could eat some
bread, I could sprinkle salt over the pig's head, I could
eat some of these thin sticks of lightly-steamed vegetable.
Then I said:

'You should get out more. Or you should read more.
Japan isn't unique—how do you think they eat in Thailand, in China, in India? Do they have one small course
after another, a stately progress from soup to sweet? No:

they sit down to an assembly of dishes and they choose from among them, which, of course, was exactly what European diners did until comparatively recently. From the Middle Ages on, service was in the form that later came to be known as *service à la française*: there were comparatively few courses—perhaps two or three—and, at each course, several dishes were set on the table and the diners chose from each what they wanted. What we're eating now is a meal served *à la russe*: more courses and less choice, most things plated in the kitchen and brought to you ready sliced up. But the fact that the Japanese don't do what we're doing now says nothing about their uniqueness. *We* weren't doing what we're doing now till well into the nineteenth century and ... ghnnn ...'

A rather tough section of pig's head had resisted my knife.

'But you've forgotten the chopsticks,' he said. 'The freedom of the meal is revealed in the chopsticks. Our knife severs, our fork punctures or holds the victim down so that the knife can tear its flesh. The chopsticks, on the other hand, are light, capricious instruments, designating the order of the meal with the simplest of gestures. It is not their job to sever or to puncture, to violate the integrity of the food ...'

But now I am somewhere else, somewhere I've never been before (damp air, a desolate garden full of statues, the aroma of eucalyptus) and an old blind man is telling me that it is no more absurd for my sad-faced friend to invent Japan than it is for me to invent him. I protest, of course, that I have done nothing so impudent: all I have done is to take certain of the sad-faced man's thoughts and rearrange them, paying as much attention to their textures and to the spaces between them as to their content.

'Exactly—just like a Japanese meal,' says the old man. 'But you'll always have Paris,' he adds, not unkindly.

# k is for kitchen

I have two fantasies of myself in the kitchen. The first is of me as the ultimate peasant cook. There I stand in some capacious proletarian garment (or an Issey Miyake version thereof), whipping up culinary wonders with the aid of just one old knife, a cast-iron pot and an open fire. The second fantasy is of me as technological *wunderkind*. The kitchen is sleek, white and metallic, and my work is largely conceptual. There's no operation for which I haven't got an appropriate machine. I've got machines to slice for me, to grind, stone and de-pip, and with them I serve up minimalist creations, elegant little purées and terrines on black plates, to svelte, dark, power-dressed women. (I realise that this fantasy is past its use-by date, but I still haven't really adjusted to the fact that nobody wears red braces or watches *Dynasty* any more.)

Of course, the point about these fantasies is that they

are *fantasies*. They have little bearing on my actual culinary practice, and you would be unwise, were you a manufacturer of kitchen equipment, to base your sales policy on anything I might say on the matter. Except, of course, at Christmas. This is the time of year when the desperate need to buy something for people who suddenly seem to have everything causes some of us to try, fatally, to turn fantasy into fact. Suppose, for example, that you and your partner like eating at the little Moroccan place on the corner. What better way of demonstrating your affection than by a seasonal presentation of a *couscousier*? Or a *tagine*? Or perhaps a *tandoor*, if you're fond of things Indian? They'll sit nicely in the kitchen next to all that other exotica you never use: the *tian*, the *marmite*, the *paella* pan.

It's probably better to look on these durables as sculpture and not to feel guilty about the fact that you never use them. After all, how often do you want couscous? And when you do want it, you can just go round to the little Moroccan place, can't you? Enjoy your freedom of choice; it is very rare. In the distant lands where all this paraphernalia is commonplace, they seldom get to eat anything other than what can be cooked with it. That, of course, is the reason why they have it: if you're going to spend the rest of your life eating couscous, it's pretty sensible to have the best gear for preparing the stuff.

The obvious explanation for this desire to fill our shelves with strangely shaped pieces of earthenware and metal is that we've been on far too many cheap holidays overseas and to far too many ethnic restaurants at home. It's possible, though, that there's a deeper reason, to be sought in the more distant past. The arrival in the mid-nineteenth century of the cast-iron stove is supposed to have been a moment of liberation for the kitchen work-force. Now, freed from the sooty tyranny of the open hearth, you could boil and simmer and bake all at once. The result, as the historian Ruth Schwartz Cowan tells us, was that the stove 'augured the death of one-pot cooking or, rather, of one-dish meals—and in doing so probably increased the amount of time that women spent in pre-paring foodstuffs for cooking.' The stove helped to lib-erate the man of the house, who no longer had to expend a lot of energy collecting fuel for an open fire, but not the woman. And also, perhaps, it set us on the path to thinking of the kitchen as a place where, given enough technological clobber, you can do more or less anything. You can boil and simmer and bake *and* make couscous, tandoori chicken and paella. The old peasant kitchen, with its single pot simmering and bubbling for most of the day, was the warm centre of the home; the modern kitchen, even when there's no wall separating it from the rest of the home, can often be just a workshop. You can treat your workshop as a grim, functional place where you unfreeze things and microwave them or you can have fun pretending to be Moroccan, but a workshop is a workshop.

It doesn't have to be like this. We, or most of us, can have couscous whenever we want it—*and* tandoori chicken *and* paella—just by going down the street or ordering in. Nothing new about this, of course: the cookshop, serving take-away puddings and the like, has a long history in Europe, and the Chinese were at it a thousand years ago. Anyway, I for one would never be able to hack it in a real peasant kitchen: everything needs to be chopped or ground relentlessly and then cooked and stirred for several hours, because what all these poor folks have plenty of is time.

All of which might suggest that the technological fantasy, rich in labour-saving devices, is the better one to pursue. For me it's certainly the sexier of the two. I read *Gourmet Traveller* or *Vogue Entertaining* much as other people read porn magazines, and those glossy enticements to buy smooth, chrome things made by European firms with alarming names like Bosch and Smeg are for me the equivalent of advertisements for vibrators, leather riding crops and ben-wa balls. I just can't get enough of all that tackle. Perhaps, I think to myself as I fervidly turn the pages, perhaps my sex life would be happier if I had a KitchenAid. It whips, mixes, shreds, kneads, minces, strains, slices, juices, extrudes pasta and stuffs sausages, and it's available in a choice of Cadillac Red or Aspen White. It must be good because its praises are sung by a well-known cook in authentic Franglais—'Chefs in many, many countries have been using KitchenAid mixers for

70 years'—though at $499 (or 'only $499' as the Franglais speaker puts it) this is hardly one for the impulse purchaser.

'It is as difficult to put together a kitchen as to create a library,' said Grimod de La Reynière, fastidiously showing up my prurience. But he was writing in the days when putting a library together was the sort of thing that gentlemen did. They didn't just throw together a bunch of books; they made sure they had what a good library ought to have: Caesar's *Commentaries*, Homer, Horace, the *Georgics* as well as the *Aeneid*, and the complete works of Bishop Bossuet. There were no discrepant elements in such collections, because they were all bound together by the Western classical tradition from which they had emerged. Similarly, Grimod's idea of a good kitchen would have been one set up to produce the roasts and *ragoûts* of eighteenth-century France. He didn't have to worry about the exotica because, for the most part, he hadn't heard of them. And he didn't have to worry about labour-saving devices because, of course, the labour in his kitchen was never his labour.

Unable to be as fastidious as Grimod, I'm left with my fantasies. Like porn magazines—some porn magazines, at any rate—they're probably harmless just so long as you remember that fantasy is all they are. The reality is time, labour, trial and error. Whenever I'm tempted to buy some plastic and metal thing that will do for me anything I might want to do with an orange short of actually eating it, I think of Anton Mossiman. He's one of the best chefs in Britain, and one of the most spectacular things I've ever seen on a television food program was the sight of him segmenting an orange. He did it with a few deft motions of one small knife. As a display of skill it was like watching Fred Astaire dance, like hearing Wynton Marsalis play. You can't buy skill like that and you can't give it away. But it's what I'd like for Christmas.

# 1 is for liquamen

It is a sad fact that political power and a serious interest in food seldom seem to go hand in hand. Or, alternatively, it's not a sad fact at all: better that people while away their time potting bergamot than that they do so plotting world domination. But, sad or not, it does seem to be a fact. What does President Clinton eat? Hamburgers. What did the British eat while they were running half the world? It scarcely bears thinking about. And what of the Mongols? Having invaded China and brought under their dominion a vast empire full of cooks and connoisseurs, they amazed their new subjects by ignoring the delicacies now available to them and sticking to the scungy stuff they'd eaten at home (a lot of mutton and mare's milk).

The Chinese themselves are something of an exception to this rule and so, of course, are the French, but

I'm not sure what to make of the Romans. On the one hand, empire gave them access to the culinary riches of most of the known world; on the other, empire brought with it boring responsibilities. It's difficult to imagine that a conscientious, hard-working local governor like Pontius Pilate would have had much time for the pleasures of the table, what with all those unruly locals to take care of and all their strange tribal customs. Something plain and evocative of home is all he'd want, I'd imagine, like some British District Commissioner of the last century tucking into Gentleman's Relish and toast after a hard day keeping up appearances in front of the natives.

Indeed, can it be mere coincidence that Gentleman's Relish has a Latin name, *Patum Peperium*, and that it bears a close resemblance to *liquamen*, a sauce much favoured by the Romans? Well, yes, a complete coincidence, actually: *liquamen* bears a close resemblance to quite a number of sauces, most of them unconnected with empire or power. Made from fermented fish, it's similar not merely to Gentleman's Relish but also to Worcestershire Sauce and the fish sauces of Asia, like the Vietnamese *nuoc mam* or the *nam pla* of Thailand.

But the very idea of rotten fish tends to arouse strong feelings. The Cajuns of Louisiana pride themselves on their omnivorousness (bumper sticker: 'Cajuns make better lovers because they eat anything') but in the 1980s even some of them were horrified to be told that their new Vietnamese neighbours ate this sort of thing. Grimod de La Reynière, their distant kinsman from nearly two centuries ago, has a recipe for an anchovy sauce, based on *liquamen* according to his English biographer (who seems rather shocked by the idea) but timorously made with fresh anchovies and therefore much milder than the real thing.

Writing in 1825, Jean Anthelme Brillat-Savarin, Grimod's successor and superior in this line of culinary literature, seems to have been unable to believe that so costly a sauce (which he calls by its other name, '*garum*') could have been made by pressing fish entrails. He suggests that it may have been an imported sauce, 'perhaps that *soy* which comes to us from India and which is known to be the result of letting certain fishes ferment with mushrooms'. Not only is this an error—fish don't come into soy sauce at all, though there is indeed a form of the stuff which is made with mushrooms—but it's an error for which there is little excuse. Soy sauce had been known in Europe for more than a hundred years by the time Brillat-Savarin wrote, so he ought to have been able to avoid this sort of fruitless speculation. Even William Dampier, writing a century and a quarter before Brillat-Savarin, knew enough to be in doubt about the matter: 'I have been told that Soy is made partly with a fishy Composition,' he said, '. . . tho' a Gentleman . . . told me that it was made only with Wheat, and a sort of Beans mixt with Water and Salt.' The anonymous gentleman was, of course, right: soy sauce is made of wheat and soya beans.

Nobody who wants to stay alive eats rotten fish. The uncontrolled microbial degradation of a foodstuff—the process we call 'rotting'—results in products that are usually disgusting to be near and dangerous to eat. In most cases, we prefer to limit or control the process; when, for example, we ferment milk to turn it into cheese, those microbes which degrade the liquid also prevent the growth of other, more dangerous, organisms. Understandably, there are few foods in which this process is allowed to go on for too long or to get out of hand, though one could mention in this context the fiercesomely toxic rotted condiments enjoyed in the Near East during the Middle Ages.

One of these condiments was known by the name of *murri*, and this, apparently, is a word foreign to Arabic, which encourages the food historian Charles Perry to speculate that it might derive from the Greek *halmyris*, 'a salty thing', and that the substance itself might be related to *garos*, the Greek version of *garum* or *liquamen*. (Perry doesn't mention the fact that the Roman sauce was also known as *muria*, which might suggest a further connection to *murri*.) But the difference between *murri* and *muria*, *garum* or *liquamen*, was that *murri* really was the product of long rotting. Moistened barley dough was left for forty days in the summer sun until it was black, then it was moistened again and left for another fortnight until it began to bubble. The liquid, strained off and flavoured with herbs and spices, was a popular addition to many dishes and an excellent source of the most virulent carcinogens.

Liquamen was an altogether safer proposition. The fish out of which it was made were fermented in copious amounts of salt, which would have inhibited microbial growth when the vessel into which they were put was left out in the sun, as it was supposed to be, for seven days.

But the myth of liquamen as something high and horrible dies hard. Not long ago, Colleen McCullough, popular novelist and chronicler of illicit passion amongst the priesthood, turned her attention to the heaving breasts and disordered togas of Julius Caesar's Rome. Thoughtfully, she provided her readers, the airline passengers of the world, with all manner of aids to comprehension: maps, appendices, and a glossary in which the (unspecified) process by which liquamen was manufactured is described as 'calculated to make a modern man or woman ill at the thought . . .' In a curious *non sequitur* McCullough adds that 'apparently it stank, being extremely concentrated'. (The poet Horace might have agreed with her, though: he writes of *muria*, 'the kind that stinks in a Byzantine jar'.)

Not even the popularity of Thai and Vietnamese food has been enough to dispel the idea that the Romans couldn't have been up to much in the kitchen if they thought that you improved things by smothering them with rotted fish (though the Thais and Vietnamese, it has to be admitted, are not as lavish with their fish sauces as the Romans appear to have been with theirs). This is just one of the popular illusions about the tucker of the Caesars. Another is that it was usually gross and that when it wasn't gross, it was over-refined: one day, flamingoes and larks' tongues; the next, whole roast boar, stuffed down so enthusiastically that you just had to get up from your couch mid-meal, gather your toga around you, and pop out for a quick vomit.

To some extent the Romans have only themselves to blame for our misconceptions. Only from their books can we learn what they ate, and in Latin literature, as in much other literature, meals are never innocent: they are iron-ised, made extravagant or disgusting for literary purposes. The guiltiest party here is undoubtedly Titus Petronius Arbiter, whose book *Satyricon* has left us with a picture of Roman vulgarity so vivid that his satiric excesses have frequently been treated as documentary fact. Trimalchio, a freed slave grown rich, is giving a dinner party, and nothing has been omitted that will surprise or delight his guests and impress upon them a sense of their host's wealth: dormice dressed with honey and poppy seeds, a wild boar surrounded by pastry pigs and filled with live thrushes, a pig stuffed with sausages and blood pudding, and, for dessert, pastry thrushes stuffed with raisins and nuts.

The dormice were neither an extravagance nor a satir-ical flourish; the Romans farmed them, and Petronius' contemporary Apicius, author of the only cookery book to have come down to us from Roman times, gives a recipe for dormouse stuffed with pork, its own meat, pine nuts and, inevitably, liquamen. In fact, though, the consumption of stuffed dormice had been expressly forbidden by law some two hundred years before Apicius, and other Romans seem to have had it in for any dish that involved stuffing things with other things. Perhaps their vision of Rome as an austere, serious republic was offended by the idea of adding meat to meat; perhaps, as one commentator suggests, stuffed animals were a literary metaphor for stuffed people gorging themselves on the plenty of empire.

How can we penetrate the fictions and ironies of Latin literature and get at what the Romans really ate? In all probability we can't. It may be, of course, that not everything we read about in the literature has literary significance; as Freud said, sometimes a cigar is just a cigar. The problem is that we can never know for certain when those times are. So it is with food. No doubt your average Roman author in the early days of the empire did sometimes sit down to a humble meal of wheat porridge and fava beans, but if he describes the meal in writing, we naturally suspect that he has a point to make. Is he perhaps trying to present a contrast between the simple pleasures of rural life and the frivolities of the city? Or is he telling us that what was good enough in the virtuous days of the republic is good enough for him? It could be that he's telling us that this is what he ate because this is what he ate; he was on his own and this was all he could find in the, as it were, fridge. After close on two thousand years, it isn't easy to tell.

Even when Cicero praises the pleasures of the table, he rather too obviously has a point to make that isn't to do with eating. How right, he says, were our ancestors to call a dinner party a *convivium*, because it means a living together. And how much better the Latin word is than those the Greeks use. Their words for the same thing mean either a drinking together or an eating together, 'thereby apparently exalting what is of least value in these associations with that which gives them their greatest charm.' Between Cicero, who thinks that the food hardly matters at all, and Trimalchio, who thinks that it matters because it's an expression of his wealth and power, there were, perhaps, some Romans who took an informed, unforced pleasure in what they ate. I like to think that Apicius was one of them. His book includes instructions on how to correct the flavour of liquamen that has developed a bad odour, and you have to respect anybody who's that serious about what so many people think is just a barrel of stinking fish.

# m is for music

Gioachino Rossini, searching for themes to use in his *Stabat Mater*, could think only of pastries and truffles. He was serious about truffles; it's difficult to think of a more serious use of them than in the dish that bears his name, *Tournedos Rossini*, where truffle joins foie gras atop the tournedos and essence of truffles appears as part of a demi-glace sauce. But Rossini did not invent *Tournedos Rossini*. The food he served to his guests, though the ingredients were often good, seems to have been renowned most of all for its lavishness; he knew enough about macaroni to impress the experts, but his famous *macaroni à la Rossini* was a terrifying edifice of leftovers piled high on the dish.

Nonetheless, Rossini, who breakfasted lightly and rarely ate lunch, seems to have been a gourmand rather than a glutton: offered abundant but simple fare at the table of the Archbishop of Florence, he was observed to eat only a slice of the roast. (George Frideric Handel, on the other hand, seems to have gone for quantity as well as, or rather than, quality: he is said to have complained about the goose that it was 'a most inconvenient bird, too much for one and not enough for two'.) But can we draw some connection between the rational pleasures of Rossini's music—witty, detached, its romanticism lightly borne up on classical pinions—and the pleasures of the food that he enjoyed so much?

There are many reasons for associating food with music, but perhaps not all that many good reasons. Why should we think that food has more to do with music than with, say, painting or literature? One reason (one bad reason) may be that when we're talking about food or about music, words fail us sooner than they do when we're talking about literature or movies. We don't very often discuss music in the way that we discuss these other arts and the reason for this is obvious: literature and movies have content—usually narrative content—and music doesn't. Like food, it isn't about anything. Even when music has words, it's the words that are about something, not the music. Sometimes, both food and music can seem to represent something—you can have an overture that purports to be about Napoleon's retreat from Moscow or a cake that's shaped and coloured like Elvis Presley—but you can usually get a long way into appreciating the product without understanding what it's supposed to be about. Somebody who'd never heard of Napoleon might enjoy listening to the *1812 Overture* and somebody blind from birth could enjoy eating a cake that was supposed to look like Elvis.

Food and music are both of them immune to paraphrase. When describing or analysing a sonata or a symphony, you can't summarise the story, because there isn't one. You have to talk about music in musical terms, and these, unfortunately, are not accessible to everyone. A feeling of dumb resentment creeps over many music lovers when they are presented with, say, an analysis of Rossini's *Barber of Seville* in terms of tonics and subdominants, cadences and sonata form. In talk about food there's less danger of such rebarbative technicality, though it would be fun to annoy a food lover by analysing *Tournedos Rossini* at a similar level of abstraction: 'Take a thin section from a hindquarter of beef, removing all the nerve and fat, subject it to direct transfer of energy at a temperature no greater than that of the lubricative medium in which the heating process is to take place, and remove it at the point of coagulation of the fibre proteins but before the gelatinisation of the collagen . . .'

The comparison is unfair. Music is a complex structure whose effects are available to all but whose complexities are best described in terms and notation which many find opaque. On the other hand, to describe a dish too abstractly is simply not to describe it at all, just as an enumeration of every bolt, cable and bit of metal that go to make up the Sydney Harbour Bridge will not amount to a description of the Sydney Harbour Bridge.

A musical score is not exactly a recipe. Certainly, it can be read as a set of instructions which, if followed correctly, will produce that sequence and synchrony of sounds which we call, say, *The Barber of Seville*. But there is a perfectly understandable sense in which the score is more than a recipe, a sense in which the opera *is* the score. *The Barber of Seville* isn't the sum of its many performances; you can know what it is and talk about it simply by being able to interpret, in your mind alone, the notation in which it is encoded.

Can the same ever be true of a recipe? Possibly: M. F. K. Fisher talks of reading ancient recipes and trying to recreate their flavours on what she nicely calls her mind's tongue, and we can perhaps imagine this being done so well that anybody possessing the skill would never actually have to taste the food itself. We can imagine it, but, if the skill exists, I don't think it is as common as the ability to read a musical score. Food, unlike music, seems essentially to involve performance.

It could be that when people think of food and music together, they are not thinking of difficult music—the preludes of Bach, the later quartets of Beethoven—that needs to be attended to with great concentration. They are thinking of music overheard, a simple sensuous pleasure, very much, perhaps, like food. The comparison is assisted by the fact that, entering as they do by different bodily orifices, music and food can be enjoyed more or less simultaneously. Or, rather, they can be more or less enjoyed more or less simultaneously. There are musical masterpieces—and a few culinary masterpieces too—that demand all our attention. I'm not amused by hosts who think it all right if Charlie Parker or the Mass in B Minor have to do battle for my attention with the banalities of their conversation or the inadequacies of the food.

There's no simple scale of values operating here. Handel's *Concerti Grossi* and Vivaldi's orchestral works are equally polite, equally capable of shimmying away at a touch of the volume control and of maintaining thereafter a discreet, Jeeveslike presence scarcely detectable above the murmur of conversation and the clatter of cutlery. I do believe, however, that they are not of equal value. If I'm right, does that mean that it's fine to use one of these composer's works as a background to your cassoulet and garden salad, but not the other's? I think not: Vivaldi is at once so vacuous and so available that to play his music at your dinner party is to give the impression that you've picked up an aerosol marked 'European High Culture' and sprayed its refined contents in a thin mist over your guests. There are other aerosols, of course—the Black-American-street-music aerosol, the citizen-of-planet-earth aerosol (pygmy songs, gamelans and dance music from South African townships)—but to use any of them is to give the impression that you've ordered in your culture, just as you might have ordered in the food.

But isn't there a history of music—and sometimes very good music—being played while people eat? Well, yes, there's Mozart's *Eine Kleine Nachtmusik* and Telemann's *Musique de Table*. But there are good reasons for thinking that Telemann himself would have been offended if his listeners had paid more attention to their chicken fricassee than to the sophisticated trios, quartets and *ouvertures* in the French style that he had laid on for them. He might in his youth have written what he called 'meat-and-gravy symphonies' for the town band, but the *Musique de Table* was serious music, intended to be played between the courses or when the meal had ended.

This has often been the way with music played at meals. In French fiction of the early middle ages the entertainment enters only when the meal is over. Later literature describes *entremets*—entertainments staged between the *mets*, or courses, while the guests still sat at table—but makes it clear that music and dancing happen after the eating has finished and the tables have been removed from the hall. This was reasonable enough, given that at this time it was common in aristocratic households in England and France for men and women to eat separately and then come together for the post-prandial entertainment. The entremets themselves could, however, be musical. At the Feast of the Pheasant, put on in 1453 by Phillip the Fair, Duke of Burgundy, the entremet was musical and aimed, one assumes, at a male audience, since the entire feast was intended as a recruiting exercise for a crusade to recapture Constantinople from the infidel. Unfortunately, Olivier de La Marche, who describes the feast, its music and its decorations in some detail, has little to say about the food other than it was very good and there was a lot of it.

This is a sad reflection of the tendency of truly serious people not to take food seriously. An eleventh-century chronicler tells us that, at meals, Adalbert, Archbishop of Hamburg, 'took delight not so much in food and wine as in witty conversation, or in the stories of kings, or in unusual doctrines of philosophers'. Dining alone, he sometimes called in players of the lute to entertain him, but only when they seemed 'necessary for alleviating his anxieties'.

The attitude displayed here may, of course, be as much that of the chronicler as of his subject, but I wonder whether this basic disdain for food and music—this tendency to treat each of them purely as a means to an end—might have its origins in Platonic philosophy. Plato, though he obviously thought music far more important than cookery, spoke of both in quite similar terms: they were mere sensual distractions, debilitating to the mind, dangerous to the body politic. He thought that music, except for the more martial kind, tended to turn men into wimps, unfit for the service of the republic; so the softening effects of melody needed to be balanced by a good work-out in the gym. As to cookery, it was not an art, he said, because it was not rational. Unlike medicine—which truly was an art because it rationally sought the good of the body—cookery was devoted not to the body's true good but only to its pleasure and gratification. It was not an art, but a mere routine, a knack.

In that great age of Platonic revival, the renaissance, food and music might play their part in political spectacle but it was music that tended to capture the attention of the intellectuals who wrote about these shows. In 1539, Cosimo I, Duke of Florence, married Eleonora, daughter of Don Pedro de Toledo, Spanish Viceroy of Naples. The event was lavishly celebrated with pageants, feasting, plays and music, all of which were lavishly described in a letter written by one Pier Francesco Giambullari. When it comes to the food, though, Signor Giambullari is a disappointment. 'The courses of the great banquet were infinite, with many sorts of food in each course,' he writes. 'I do not describe the particulars in order not to lose time for such an unimportant thing; it is enough to say that there lacked nothing appropriate to such a high prince.' He then goes on to describe the floor show which followed the meal—eight madrigals performed by elaborately costumed singers—in the greatest detail.

In China at about the same time, they ordered these things very differently. The regulations for banquets at the Ming court included the music with which, in the course of the feast, the praises of the imperial ancestors were to be sung. *Yu-shih-yueh*, 'music to encourage eating', it was called, and it was performed by a chorus from the

Office of Music. When the music was to be played and when it was to be silent, when the guests were to stand and when they were to sit, when the dancers were to dance and when the food was to be served—every detail was elaborately plotted.

Even in the West, food and music could, just occasionally, form part of an integrated entertainment. The Florentine philosopher Marsilio Ficino (a Platonist if ever there was one) argued that a banquet should refresh all the parts of man: the body, the senses and the reason. At a banquet with musical accompaniment, the body was renewed while the mind was moved by earthly echoes of celestial harmony. In 1475, celestial harmony beguiled the guests at the wedding banquet of Costanzo Sforza and Camilla d'Aragon. Here, the central conceit was that the whole thing had been laid on by the Olympian gods: Jove, for example, furnished roast meat and cooked peacocks; Neptune, not surprisingly, provided the fish. The presentation of the food was choreographed and the courses were interspersed with music, dance and allegorical mime. More than two centuries later, no less a dignitary than the commander of the King's Musketeers, d'Artagnan (a real person whom the genius of Alexandre Dumas has made irredeemably fictional), rode into a courtyard at Versailles at the head of a parade in which Apollo, the four ages of man, the hours of the day and the signs of the zodiac were all represented. They were all followed by a ballet in which the four seasons entered bearing

127

platters of food. Each of the seasons had twelve followers carrying seasonal delicacies.

The music for this extravaganza—known as 'The Pleasures of the Enchanted Isle' and held to celebrate the installation of Louise de La Vallière as the official mistress of Louis XIV—was by Jean-Baptiste Lully, one of the greatest composers of the French baroque. Some of it survives and can be enjoyed today on CD in performances meticulously researched and stylishly delivered on original instruments. Listening to the suave tones of Lully's music, as fresh today as when they were written, one cannot help wondering whether we might take historical reconstruction a little further: could we ever hope to reproduce the food as well, or any such ancient food, with similar regard for authenticity?

At first sight (or taste, or hearing) early cooking ought to be at least as bright a possibility as early music. Sadly, it fades a little, just a little, on closer inspection. Although, as I've said, a musical score is more than a recipe, it is, nonetheless, still a sort of recipe; it is a set of instructions. But instructions speak only to those who know how to interpret them. If you don't know what a dish is supposed to look like or how it is supposed to taste, a recipe will not help you much, and here the cook is even worse off than the musician.

In 1707, twenty years after Lully's death, Jacques Hottetterre le Romain wrote a book on the *Principles of the Flute, Recorder and Oboe*. Hottetterre's book remains an important text for anyone who wants to interpret the music of this period. He tells his readers not merely how to play the notes but how to play them with style, how to spice them up (as any contemporary instrumentalist would have been expected to do) with little turns of phrase like the *porte-de-voix*, the *coullement* and the *double cadence*. Moving briskly through the basics, Hotteterre is a conscientious teacher, aware of the difficulties of trying to impart skill though the medium of print. 'Although many people are of the opinion that the embouchure cannot be taught by rules, there *are* some rules which will be extremely helpful for you in finding out how to do it,' he writes. 'The advice of a good teacher to supplement the demonstration can save much time and trouble to those who wish to acquire this embouchure.' And he ends his book with what is, for me, a tantalising sentence: 'If, in spite of the care I have taken to make these principles understandable, anyone should find any difficulties in them; I will always be pleased and honoured to clear them up for them, where I live at rue Christine, in Monsieur Royer's House.' These are poignant words for us now. They acknowledge the inadequacy of verbal instruction and they offer further help, but it is help of which in the nature of things we cannot avail ourselves.

This is frustrating enough but, when it comes to early cooking, things are considerably worse. You've got an old cookery book, published centuries ago, and you've got some raw ingredients that might or might not resemble those familiar to the book's long-dead author. (More probably, they will not be much like the old ingredients: modern breeding and feeding techniques have transformed our produce.) At least if you're playing early music like Lully's you have two people trying to help you: Lully, who wrote the stuff, and Hotteterre, who is trying to tell you how to interpret it. Lully's notation may, it's true, now seem a little opaque and Hotteterre's words may be less than adequate, but, on the whole, life looks just a little less lonely for the musician than for the cook.

Recently, a very successful English cook confessed that his first attempts at certain Italian dishes were hampered by the fact that they were based only on book learning, so he didn't know whether pasta and chickpeas were meant to be served wet and sloppy or dry. But at least he was able eventually to visit Italy. I don't know if the rue Christine is still there or, if it is, whether M. Royer's house still stands, but I do know that we cannot knock on any door and expect it to be answered by Jacques Hotteterre le Romain, or indeed by La Varenne, Carême, Escoffier or any of the great cooks of old.

# n is for nature

These days, if you're interested in food, you just have to want to be Italian. It's obligatory, there's no choice. Sure, you can enjoy Peking duck, if you like, or sashimi or tom yam goong, but Italy alone provides the total culinary culture to which we're all supposed to aspire. Italian food has about it an air of spontaneity, a sense of leaving well enough alone, of doing honour to the ingredients, of long lunches under the vines, red wine, good bread to mop up the sauces. 'It is an honest cooking, too; none of the sham Grande Cuisine of the International Palace Hotel,' wrote Elizabeth David, in what can now be read as the opening of the Italian sales pitch. This was *A Book of Mediterranean Food*, first published in the dingy England of 1950, and, though, as the title indicates, it embraces the whole region, Italy has always been of all Mediterranean countries the one dearest to the hearts of the English-speaking world. From Shakespeare's comedies to *A Room with a View* (the book and the movie) and beyond, we've looked to Italy to provide us with sunlit images of a relaxed, sensual way of life that seldom seems to be on offer locally.

Born in England, this longing for the sunny south has been exported to the United States—where Thomas Jefferson gave his house an Italian name and they now make romantic movies about the Mafia—and even to Australia, which is both southern and sunny. Different eras have found different things in Italy: to the Elizabethans, it offered the best stories, the best music, the best architecture; to the Victorians, romantic views and classical ruins; to us, nothing half so cultured: all we're looking for is the natural way to a long life. And, in the last decade or so, we've found it.

Research in the 1960s showed that the populations of the Mediterranean region lived longer than people in Northern Europe and the States. They had lower rates of heart disease and of many kinds of cancer, and this despite poor standards of health care and an alarming fondness for tobacco. Early on, the idea that they had their genetic inheritance to thank for this was rejected: Mediterranean people who migrated north or to the States, and adopted the local lifestyle, quickly lost the advantages enjoyed by those who stayed behind. So perhaps it was something they ate. Before long, the things they ate came to be subsumed under the phrase 'Mediterranean diet'.

The Mediterranean diet has been fashionable in nutritional circles for some time now, but what exactly is it? Attempts at definition have yielded not one diet but many, each determined by different economic, religious, climatic and geographic factors. Even within Italy itself, there can be enormous variations in diet. Italy was not always a land swimming in olive oil: before the Second World War it was butter in the north, pork fat in the centre and olive oil only in the impoverished south. Now, it seems, the rich pleasures of *osso bucco* are losing their appeal in the north, and Milanese families which once would have got through a single bottle of olive oil in a year are now cooking with it all the time. Like us, they think that they ought to be eating a Mediterranean diet.

In the face of these complexities, a few nutritionists have suggested that we should be eating something they call an 'Optimal Traditional Mediterranean Diet'. This ideal regime contains plentiful fruit, vegetable, legumes and grains. Olive oil is its principal fat. It allows you lean red meat, but only a few times a month or in very small amounts. It involves low or moderate consumption of dairy products, fish and poultry, and moderate consumption of wine. Defenders of the idea point out that olive trees are cultivated along the entire perimeter of the Mediterranean sea and that versions of this diet, are to be found—or were to be found—in Greece and in parts of the Balkans, the Iberian peninsula, Southern France, North Africa and the Middle East.

No doubt this is all very desirable, but it sounds fishy to me. 'Optimal' presumably means 'approved by modern nutritional science', and can it really be said that there's anything truly traditional about a tradition that's acceptable only when modern nutritional science has awarded it a seal of approval? The whole idea of a Mediterranean diet that's optimal and traditional is the clumsy offspring of a marriage between scientific objectivity and advertising, because advertising is what all this Mediterranean stuff amounts to. The diet may be, most certainly is, good for us; it may have something to do with what people, at least poor people, eat—or, more likely, used to eat—on the shores of that poisoned sea; but the desire to hang on at all costs to the words 'traditional' and 'Mediterranean' comes of an advertising man's perception of what the public wants.

It was there, really, in what Elizabeth David said back in 1950: 'It is an honest cooking, too; none of the sham Grande Cuisine of the International Palace Hotel.' It's honest, it's traditional, and though some of it may be French, it's not posh French. As we all know, French chefs are nasty and arrogant and horrid; they charge too much, they blow up Greenpeace ships, and, above all, they muck food about. The French twist and torture their ingredients and disguise them with sauces; their food speaks of human artifice. Italian food speaks, sings, of Nature.

Whenever anybody tries to sell you something by

telling you that it's natural, the appropriate reaction is deep scepticism. Nature is not on anybody's side. Each species seeks to propagate itself to the fullest possible extent: with your cooperation if possible, over your dead body if necessary. The sensation of fiery heat that you experience when you tuck into a Thai curry is the chilli's way of warning you off; it just happens to be bad luck for *Capsicum frutescens* that you and I are intelligent enough to know that it can't do us any harm and perverse enough to enjoy its attempts.

The use of Nature as an advertising concept is not new. In 1869, Catherine E. Beecher and her sister Harriet Beecher Stowe (author of *Uncle Tom's Cabin*) invoked nature in their attempts to sell the idea of cooking with an open fire, as opposed to the new-fangled stoves: 'Warming by an open fire is nearest to the natural mode of the Creator, who heats the earth and its furniture by the great central fire of heaven, and sends cool breezes to our lungs.' At least the Beecher sisters had the good sense to invoke not just nature but also God, who is supposed to be on our side. Later salespeople were not always so consistent. Vegetarians have often ignored the savage, carnivorous instincts that nature has given us while at the same time arguing that by abstaining from animal flesh, we place ourselves at peace with the natural world. This is the same natural world—benign, harmonious, uncorrupted by human science and society—that you meet on labels in the health food store. Often, the products thus labelled don't at first glance look very natural, unless little boxes full of pills and powders grow on trees.

They knew a lot about nature in the Middle Ages and, of course, enjoyed celebrating its beauties in song and story; but for those few who could afford to eat well, food was a celebration of artifice, not of nature. This was a cuisine of strong contrasts and disguises. Similarly, the Japanese like to think of their cuisine as natural—and indeed they have a far greater respect for seasonality than most of us have—but by the time it gets onto the plate, their food is natural only in a very particular, very Japanese way. As Donald Richie puts it, 'in food as in landscape gardens and flower arrangements, the emphasis is on a presentation of the natural rather than the natural itself.'

The Mediterranean diet, as served up to us in restaurants and cookery books, is just that: a presentation of the natural. It is, or should be, delicious and healthy, but it's a fabrication, put together out of some of the things that the poor people of the Mediterranean used to consume because they couldn't afford red meat. It is as Italian and as natural as Beatrice and Benedick, Don Corleone, canned spaghetti and just about every pizza you're ever likely to eat.

# O is for offal

Sometimes one is told of an obscure restaurant in a foreign city that it's where the locals eat. This is supposed to be a recommendation, but frequently it isn't. For one thing, it's not exactly news: if you haven't heard of the place then it's odds on that other visitors won't have heard of it either, so who could possibly be left to go there apart from locals and tourists who've lost their guidebooks? As to the food: it's possible that the locals are in attendance because it is here, and not in the sumptuous uptown eateries, that the true, unadulterated indigenous cuisine is to be found. It's also possible that they eat here because they can't afford to eat anywhere better.

Often, the real reason for going to such places is not that you want to eat what the locals eat but that you want to watch them eating it. You want to pretend that you are not what you probably are, a tourist, but a visitor, a sympathetic and inquiring observer of native mores. This is more or less why we went to Deannie's, and we got what we wanted.

Deannie's is where the locals go for large quantities of plain, unadorned seafood—battered fish and boiled crustacean—and, since the locality in question is a suburb of New Orleans, it comes as something of a relief to the visitor to be able to see the fish plain for once and not swamped in an etouffée or gumbo. The best-known crustacean in these parts is the crawfish, caught wild in the Atchafalaya Basin and farmed throughout Cajun country, and the crawfish (which if it were Australian would be called a yabby) can be a problem. 'To peel a crawfish, a person must have an understanding of its anatomy and a willingness to see and suck its unclean, inedible parts as well as its edible parts,' says the anthropologist C. Paige Guttierez. 'Sucking the head requires the diner to put the inedible, life-like head, which later becomes part of the garbage, directly into his mouth.' The locals love to watch visitors brace themselves, dive in and do it wrong, or refuse to do it at all. Our own fumblings brought to our table a drunken man from Memphis, Tennessee. He stumbled over (reeking, as it happens, rather more of cheap aftershave than of liquor), seized one of our crawfish and lectured us about it.

'What you have to do is, you have to bust their little butts first,' he explained. 'You have to rip the head of this little sucker right here—mind, you jerk its little fucking head off right here. And you go—' He jerked its little fucking head off and slurped noisily. 'God damn that was good,' he said, his accent turning Hispanic, or perhaps it was meant to be Cajun. 'And then what you do is, you put your little finger right up on his little tail ass and then you get a *muniscule* piece of meat. You've got to do this, and if you don't do this—' He lowered his voice to a hoarse whisper. '*You have no nuts, man.*'

Ain't no doubt about it: real men suck crawfish. Of course, this wouldn't count as a proof of *cojones* if it were not for the fact that many people, and American people in particular, recoil from the idea of sucking on anything that looks too obviously like a creature that was alive and is now dead. In Australia, Britain and the States, people who would rather die on the job than be thought sexually repressed will nonetheless happily admit to all manner of gastronomic repressions: they won't eat small birds, or fish with their heads on or offal (we won't go into the insect question, interesting though it is). The boozy bravado of the man from Memphis was made possible by the squeamishness of the society in which he lived. By contrast, Mme. Z. Guinaudeau, author of *Fez: Traditional Moroccan Cooking*, is able to approach a sheep's head without getting drunk first. It's true that she refers to the cleaned-out head as 'this pitiful mask', but the rest of her instructions are briskly encouraging: 'The part much appreciated is the eye. You insert a finger delicately in the socket; a quick turn of the nail and the orb will fall out, extricate it and eat well seasoned with salt and cumin.'

I was lucky enough to be inoculated from an early age against prejudice on these matters. In our house, the giblets of chicken or turkey were not used for stock but, rather wastefully perhaps, given to me to eat cold. Off a small plate I could pick at a fascinating array of textures and flavours, hard, soft, meaty, bitter. The only piece I didn't get was that fatty part of the rear known in England as the 'parson's nose' and in Catholic Australia as the 'pope's nose'. Loving it so much herself, my mother never let on to me how good it tastes, and I don't blame her.

Various explanations have been offered for Anglo-Saxon choosiness when it comes to the animal body. Sometimes it's suggested that offal is of low social standing because it's looked upon as the food of the poor. This may well be true, but how did it become so low-rent in the first place? As the anthropologist Marshall Sahlins has pointed out, 'there is much more steak to the cow than there is tongue', so rarity value alone ought to have secured higher status for the tongue. Sahlins suggests that his fellow white Americans don't like to eat anything that's close to them. Dogs and horses are members of the family, so they don't get eaten, and when Americans do eat the muscle tissue of other animals, they fool themselves about its true nature by calling it 'meat', 'steak' or whatever. The internal parts, however, are known frankly as what they are: heart, tongue, kidney, liver (though when they're cooked some of them become 'sweet-breads'). Unlike steaks and chops, innards tend also to look alarmingly like the internal organs they are, perhaps even like human internal organs; middle-class white America is revolted by the idea of eating them— it would feel too much like cannibalism—and so it leaves them to the poor, both black and white. The low standing of offal is confirmed by the status of the people who eat it.

Sahlins hasn't quite covered every angle—would you be able to tell that cooked brains were brains if the menu hadn't told you so?—but his account may be the best we're likely to get of this mysterious prejudice. With very little modification, it can be exported to Australia, to Britain, but not, of course, to any of those nations with culinary traditions that we're supposed to respect.

A friend once gave me a cutting from a French maga-zine. It's an advertisement for pork and it depicts in full colour a number of joints and cuts. This in itself is signif-icant—you don't see many joints of meat round my way, where the butchers' windows are all full of little some-things already rolled, sliced or marinated—but what really takes the breath away is the manner in which all this meat has been displayed. No compromises here at all: it's been rearranged to look like a whole pig that has been brutally dissected, and a few knives and cleavers strategically placed leave you in no doubt as to what has gone on. A couple of earthenware pots are there as well, presumably containing

*141*

pork fat, and—the crowning touch that carries talent into the sphere of genius—the head has been wedged back into place too. It's turned towards the camera and would be looking right at us if it had eyes; but it has no eyes, only a couple of red-rimmed slits.

I doubt whether there is any English-speaking country in which you could get away with an advertisement like that (and I'm told that the French tolerance for this sort of thing is diminishing). Our advertisements show us live animals (usually schematised in the form of ready red roosters and the like) or they show us dead animals, but any suggestion that the one will eventually become the other is strictly not allowed. Usually, the dead don't look as though they were ever alive—instead, they look like sausages or pies—and the live animals don't look as though they are likely ever to be dead. But it was not always thus. Consider how S. H. Benson made Bovril a household name.

Benson was a Bovril man alright; before setting up on his own as an 'advertiser's agent', he had been employed by John Lawson-Johnston, founder of Johnston's Fluid Beef. The problem, now that Johnston's Fluid Beef was to be marketed as Bovril, was to get it into the public's head that there was something essentially beefy about the product. This was, remember, a world in which even city dwellers could still see sheep and cattle being driven through the streets to the market or the slaughterhouse. It was a world in which milk still came slopping home in pails. It was a world which had not yet made the mental separation between the supposed qualities of the animal—the strength of the bull, the maternal benevolence of the cow—and the virtues of the food that came from the animal. It was certainly not a world in which you could sell a beef extract to people by telling them that it was a good source of iron, riboflavin and niacin.

Benson tried hyperbole ('The Glory of a Man is his Strength') and he tried downright bloody cheek ('The Two Infallible Powers: the Pope and Bovril') but his boldest stroke was probably a poster that first appeared in the year 1896. It depicts a jar of Bovril and, next to it, staring at it, realistically painted, a bull with a tear in its eye. The caption is, 'Alas! My Poor Brother.' Benson's company kept the Bovril account for the next seventy years.

It's a cruel advertisement, of course, and so is one of its successors—'I hear they want more Bovril,' says one nervous-looking bull to another in a poster of 1903—but there is something odd about its cruelty. If cattle really were capable not only of grieving for their slaughtered brethren but also of articulating that grief, then you wouldn't be able to eat beef extract, would you? No, and nor would the original poster's intended audience.

There is a curious closing off of the imagination presupposed by this poster. It invites you to imagine a talking, grieving bull but it assumes that you will refrain from imagining how a talking, grieving bull would suffer on its way to the abattoir. The only explanation I can think of is that the poster was created by and for people who had not yet worked out how they felt about bulls and beef extract. They were sufficiently removed from a traditional world to be happy with beef that came in little jars, but sufficiently close to it to need to be told that this dark brown goo really was beef. They had yet to work out the moral status of the bull.

Of course, once they did work out how they felt about the bull, they decided that bulls, dead or grieving, were not what they wanted to think about when eating beef extract. So the Bovril advertisement—which looks as though it's being very frank about the origins of the product—is, in fact, not far from modern Anglo-Saxon squeamishness. The French advertisement, on the other hand, is refreshingly candid. You want pork? Fine, that involves killing pigs. But then the French are serious about their food.

In societies less committed than the French to the pleasures of the table any affirmation of the truth about what we eat is likely to have about it an air of in-your-face self-consciousness. Take, for example, one of the finest meals I have ever eaten. The scene is the (then) Australian National Gallery in Canberra and the diners are various interested parties (about eighty in number) who are in town for a conference on gastronomy. The room is long and narrow: on one side a red wall, on the other windows overlooking the sculpture garden, and down the centre a long table covered in tripe: the stomachs of many dead animals, raw, unbleached and smelly: a pitted, undulating, lunar landscape of black and brown and dirty white. We sit down nervously. Fortunately, nobody is asking us to eat uncooked tripe; it's rolled up and removed by waiters whose torsos are wrapped in white bandages.

The first course arrives: beef tartare—raw meat and raw eggs—and then the second: a beef consommé of superb depth, richness and clarity accompanied by marrow bones piled high in baskets set along the centre of the table. You poke the marrow out yourself with a knife.

Fish skin, fried very crisp, is next: a passé thing to eat according to one of my fellow diners who tells me that they were doing it in New York a few years ago. Perhaps, but I've never had it before and some banqueters don't have it now: they spurn the skin just as they have already spurned the raw meat and the bones. The next couple of courses give them something else they can't eat: the best blood sausage I've ever had, better by far than any of the black puddings of my British childhood, followed by pigeon breasts surrounded by pigeon and duck hearts. Here, though, their ordeal ends and another begins. We have some fresh goat's cheese in puff pastry and then the waiters blindfold us. There are many nervous giggles as we sit in the darkness, some fearing the return of the tripe.

It isn't tripe, though, that greets us when the blind-folds are removed, but muscatel grapes, running all the way up the middle of the table and covering the centre-piece, which is a young girl. An uncooked young girl; a live one, in fact, the daughter of restaurateur Gay Bilson, who has devised the meal.

Only now do they give us menus, and only now can we read that what we've eaten, or have just watched other people eating, has been (and I quote from the minimalist text): 'Stomach, Egg, Flesh, Bone, Skin, Blood, Heart, Milk, Fruit, Virgins' Breasts, Dead Men's Bones.' Actually, we haven't yet had the virgins' breasts or the dead men's bones; they turn out (this is something of relief) to be biscuits served with the coffee. So eating the body, and presumably the female body, has been the point of the exercise. This is why the wine has all been red and the meal so unyieldingly fleshly: hardly any vegetables except for a tiny salad with the fish skins, some apples and calvados with the sausage and some caramelised red cabbage with the pigeon.

A lot of those present were not at all pleased, some were disgusted, some felt sick, some were vegetarians. They could hardly complain at the cooking, superbly executed by Gay Bilson's chef at Berowra Waters Inn, Janni Kyritsis. What they didn't like, I presume, was so much meat and *such* meat: so many clear reminders of animality and death. In a way, their violent antipathy to this witty and beautiful banquet was as good a reaction to it as any; being revolted by it was a way of treating it with the seriousness it deserved.

I really enjoyed the whole thing, and it's hardly Gay Bilson's fault that, just once or twice in the course of the meal, its superb bravado distantly evoked for me the taste of crawfish and the aroma of cheap aftershave.

# p is for politics

There is a graffito on a wall in Pompeii which reads, 'The man with whom I do not dine is a barbarian to me.' It just goes to show how mural literature has declined since the high days of the Roman Empire (along with oratory and the art of throwing Christians to lions). One can't imagine any modern wielder of the aerosol coming up with something as thoughtful as this or, for that matter, as smug.

To a citizen of the Roman Empire, a barbarian was somebody beyond the reach of civility; to the anonymous graffitist of Pompeii, anyone who—for whatever reason and whatever his status—was beyond the reach of one's own civility might just as well have been a barbarian. We'll never know who this ancient scrawler was, but I like to imagine him not as some first-century equivalent of a kid on rollerblades wearing a baseball hat back to front but instead as a distant ancestor of Lady Bracknell. She, it will be remembered, thought that Liberal Unionists counted as Tories. 'They dine with us,' she said, in proof of her observation. 'Or come in the evening at any rate.'

By our choice of dinner partners, we mark out some important social boundaries. Beyond the dining room lie uncharted wastelands where none but barbarians dwell; within is a kingdom peopled by the subjects of our choice. The Romans recognised this: to them, the host of a dinner was its *rex*, its king, and though the title derived innocently enough from that of the *rex sacrorum*, who presided over religious sacrifices, it was an uneasy reminder of the ancient enemies of republican equality.

But though the guest list is still an instrument of power, the political significance of the table itself has altered over the years. In former times, European and Australian meals were served *à la française*: a large number of dishes were placed on the table at once and the diners took their choice from what was before them. Our way of eating, *à la russe*, was sufficiently unfamiliar in the Australia of the 1860s for Edward Abbot to devote a paragraph of the first Australian cookery book to an explanation of it: 'The dishes are placed on the side-table, and the servants carve and hand round what is required.' Now that the servants were handing round the plates (it's the servants in my house, of course, and no doubt in yours too) the guests were relieved of one or two social duties. When a table was set *à la française* not everything was within everybody's reach and the diners had to help each other to food. In France, the stiff etiquette of Louis XIV's day governed even such commonplace exchanges as these: social status dictated who got first pickings at a dish, and a man who served food to a woman of higher rank than himself tipped his hat to her before he did so.

Service *à la russe* has put an end to most of this sort of thing, though someone has to be served first, of course, and books of etiquette used to lay down elaborate orders of precedence. Nonetheless, Edward Abbot did not welcome the innovation: 'The table has a pleasing appearance, but it is scarcely a favourite mode for an Englishman, who likes to see the cut taken from the dish.' Is this English empiricism or Australian scepticism? Whatever it is, it's an odd comment, indicating, perhaps, a relative unfamiliarity with the new ways. Dining *à la russe* didn't mean that the diner couldn't see the cut taken from the dish: the art of carving, though in terminal decline, was not yet dead in Abbot's day.

Once carving ceased to be the priority of servants, it became a symbol by which the host, or perhaps the guest of honour, expressed his kingly power. One is not surprised to learn that the right to carve was distributed according to social rank in the France of *le roi soleil*, but the same was true even in republican Holland. The long, elaborate feasts which the Dutch militia enjoyed at this time (and which furnished such comforting substitutes for actual military prowess) were governed by an elaborate protocol. In the company of St George in Haarlem, the second-in-command had charge of the knife, and there was no shortage of instructional manuals to tell him what to do with it. Carving was just one of the formalities. Who poured the wine? Who sat where? These were not trivial matters: the banquet was an elaborate ritual, flamboyant and lavish, which preserved social and martial hierarchy while at the same time reinforcing the members' sense of solidarity and brotherhood.

But, of course, the militia were defining their togetherness by excluding others. Inevitably, their ostentatious and expensive displays of comradeship incurred the resentment of the barbarians without, and some Dutch towns passed sumptuary laws to limit the duration of these banquets. Laws against sumptuousness were nothing new: the Romans had them, and—unlike the Dutch, who usually forbade extravagance only when times were hard—they, or some of them, insisted that frugality was a matter of principle, not of expedience. True Roman virtue, they thought, disdained luxury and waste. Luxury enfeebled the citizens, and how would an enfeebled populace defend its liberties and laws? If you were a slave to material things, you were likely, sooner or later, to become a slave pure and simple. Better to stick to a modest diet—'the fruits of the earth, vine, and tree'—and leave the gross overeating, or the delicate sauces or the things stuffed with other things, to the craven, prostituted subjects of foreign tyrants. Hence the sumptuary

*151*

laws of 181 BC. Not only did these tell the citizens what
they weren't allowed to eat—'running to pages in their
detail and stretching to all kinds of unheard-of delights
in the process', as one historian points out—but they
even stipulated how they were to eat. Law-abiding
Romans were to dine with their front doors open, so that
their fellow citizens could see what they were eating.

This throwing open of the private realm to the public
gaze has a Maoist air to it, and with good reason: the
traditions of republican puritanism stretch all the way
from Rome to the Jacobins of revolutionary France, and
from them to Marx and his later Chinese disciples. In the
1920s, the Communists of the Peasants Association in
Hunan province forbade sumptuous feasts: no bamboo
shoots, kelp or lentil noodles in Shao-Shan; only eight
dishes at banquets in Hengshan county; in the East Three
District in Li-ling county only five, and in the West Third
District no New Year Feasts at all. I don't know whether
any of this really hurt, but it certainly meant something:
the Chinese have always been very alive to the cultural
and political significance of food, and, in imperial times,
food played an essential role in the rituals of the court.
During the Ming dynasty, elaborate regulations distinguished four degrees of imperial banquet—the great, the
medial, the normal, the minor—and laid down the order
of precedence with which the guests were to enter and
be seated; social degree or official position determined
each diner's proximity to the imperial table.

With their orders of precedence and their rules for seating, the imperial banquets emphasised the emperor's place at the centre of things. The emperor was the standard against which all else was to be measured. But even without such an imperial measure, any social ordering or ranking of food will be enough to give you politicised eating. Something like fifty years ago, the French food writer Curnonsky wrote in some detail about the political and class allegiances of the dinner table: the extreme right favoured classical *haute cuisine*, the centrists preferred plain country food, *gauchistes* liked something a little more exotic, and so on. He was joking, of course, but it's a very French joke. It depends for its plausibility on the existence of a high cuisine, a classical tradition against which everything else can be measured. What matters to Curnonsky is not so much the fact that the bourgeoisie and the intellectual left differ from each other but that both differ from the upper-class right. Take the posh food away and the whole structure collapses, which is why you couldn't do a Curnonsky on the Australian diet, in which, by and large, posh food *is* exotic food.

In fact, it doesn't quite work in France, either: at least not if you want to take Curnonsky's categories from the dinner table to the broader political arena. As Curnonsky recognised, classical *haute cuisine* was an expensive business. It demanded chefs so skilled and ingredients so good that only embassies and palaces could afford to do it well; what hotels offered was often just a parody of the real thing. And we all know what sort it is who eat in embassies and palaces, and, for that matter, in hotels: international types, cosmopolitan people, rich financiers without a homeland whose only allegiance is to their money and their transcontinental tribe. Jews, in fact. The notion of the Jew as rootless cosmopolitan is as important to fascist as to Stalinist mythology, which is why the extremes of left and right could unclench their fists and join hands in condemnation of the sort of expensive swill that rich Jews were said to guzzle on their international travels. Only twenty years or so before Curnonsky wrote his witty *jeu d'esprit*, French fascists were echoing the Nazis in their suspicion of the noisy, fickle, cosmopolitan world in which *haute cuisine* was served. Like the Nazis (and, for that matter, the republican Romans), they seem to have been altogether suspicious of food and, also like the Nazis, they favoured simplicity: the one-pot dish—*pot au feu* in France, *eintopf* in Germany—around which the family, basic unit of fascist society, would gather in communal celebration of true, indigenous traditions.

This sinister sentimentality of the extreme right is by no means dead. The high cuisine of embassies and hotels is probably no longer much of a problem for your modern fascist, but foreign food certainly is. In Europe, the neo-fascist nostril is always being assailed by the spicy stench of immigrant cooking (one assumes that for the British, the preferred Aryan aroma is that of boiled cabbage). Of course, they, not being very bright, have mistaken their enemy: it's not *garam masala* or *Imam bayildi* that they should be worrying about, but commercial fast food.

A few years ago, Professor Bruce Kraig suggested that the hot dog was the perfect symbol of American multiculturalism. The dog itself was the universal, the bland substrate which united all ethnicities and upon which each culture could work its own peculiar variations: the kosher hot dog of Jewish New York, the deep-fried dog of the South, the chilli dog of the south-west.

If there's any dish capable of serving the same amiable purpose in Australian society, it has to be the pizza, a bland circle of dough topped, according to taste (or the lack of it), with tomatoes, anchovies, egg and bacon, satay sauce or something involving chunks of pineapple. Of course, one is tempted—God, how one is tempted!—to dismiss with patrician disdain those people who like ham and pineapple on their pizzas, but it's worth withholding the full force of one's contempt just long enough for a little reflection. In a good pizza place, taste is truly democratic. Everybody eats the same dough, and the difference between the full Hawaiian works and what I would regard as a good topping (a bit of tomato, a bit of peperoni) is more one of preference than of price.

Nobody is king when we eat pizza. Nobody carves, nobody gets the best bit, there is no point on the circumference from which the most succulent cut is taken. You could, of course, say the same of the *pot au feu* or the *eintopf,* but they, while establishing a democracy around the table, also exclude the uninvited, the barbarians. The pizza, on the other hand, is subtle; it moves easily between the public realm and the private. Just look at a pizza restaurant: some people are eating there, others are waiting for take-aways that they will eat privately at home with family and friends, but everybody eats much the same sort of thing. Even if you stay at home and dial out for your pizzas, you are still eating a dish that has crossed boundaries. Your meal is private, but not in the exclusive sense celebrated by Lady Bracknell, and what you eat is public food, but not in the sense enforced by the Roman sumptuary laws. Born amongst the Neapolitan poor, gathering to itself the culinary traditions of the whole world, the modern pizza is, for all its shortcomings, the gastronomic symbol of our political maturity.

# q is for qualia

The image that many people have of philosophers as unworldly creatures, socially inept, nerdish in dress and manner, strangers to the more refined pleasures of the senses, is a malicious caricature—made all the more malicious by the fact that it is, in very many cases, entirely accurate. The great Ludwig Wittgenstein, whose best work has a breathtakingly beautiful, cold perfection, said that he didn't mind what he ate providing it was always the same. Socrates thought that all cooks were essentially shysters; their supposed knowledge wasn't real knowledge at all, because it did not rationally promote the health of the body.

Fortunately, it has recently emerged that Plato (whose writings tell us what Socrates said or should have said) did leave us a dialogue in which Socrates turns his attention to issues of food and flavour. The dialogue addresses questions that today are perhaps even more important than they were in ancient Athens: What is flavour? How many kinds of flavour are there? How can we communicate our experience of flavour to others? It is an interesting document for a number of reasons: it establishes that Greek philosophers of Socrates' day believed, as we do, that there are only four basic flavours (though Plato's pupil Aristotle thought there were eleven) and it contains the earliest known reference to pickled beetroot, which has not hitherto been recognised as a constituent of fourth-century Athenian sandwiches.

Most of the Socratic dialogues draw their titles from one of their participants, usually the one to whom Socrates has given the most thorough intellectual duffing-up. In this case, though, it seems appropriate to name the dialogue after its subject matter and to call it by the philosophical word for the subjective experience of the qualities of the material world: 'qualia'.

SOCRATES:    Good evening, Alcibiades.

ALCIBIADES:    Oh, it's you.

SOCRATES:    You are going in to the dinner party, are you?

ALCIBIADES:    I most certainly am. What's it to you, Socrates?

SOCRATES:    Just asking. Why should I mind?

ALCIBIADES:    There's no reason at all why you should mind, but you probably will. You always

do. No matter what I want to do—no
matter what any normal, sensible
Athenian citizen wants to do—you find
some philosophical reason to object
to it.

SOCRATES: This is unfair, Alcibiades.

ALCIBIADES: Unfair my arse.

SOCRATES: Argued like a true philosopher, Alcibiades. But, since you raise the question,
why *are* you going to the dinner party?

ALCIBIADES: For fun. Remember fun, Socrates?

SOCRATES: Rational pleasure—

ALCIBIADES: No, not rational pleasure—fun. Do you
ever ask yourself why you don't get
invited to dinner parties any more? It's
because you're not fun. It's always the
same with you: just as everybody's getting
seriously into some great issue of the day,
like why Aristophanes isn't as funny as he
used to be or why we scored fewer gold
medals than Sparta in the Olympics, you
chime in with some blockbuster like
'What is the nature of the Good?' People
don't like that sort of thing. It makes
them feel stupid.

SOCRATES: You surprise me, Alcibiades, because I
confess that when I go out to dinner, it
is I who feel stupid.

ALCIBIADES:   OK, fine, I'll buy it. I mean, it's not like
              I'm in a hurry or anything, is it? Here we
              go, then—and Plato, if you're listening
              behind that Ionic column, this is where
              you start taking notes, dear—why do you
              feel stupid, O Socrates?

SOCRATES:     Because it is always clear that everybody
              at the meal knows more than I.

ALCIBIADES:   Well, when it comes to, say, dress sense
              or the Olympics, they probably do.

SOCRATES:     No, I am referring to the food and the
              drink. They speak as though knowledge
              about these matters was possible and they
              say things I do not understand.

ALCIBIADES:   Such as?

SOCRATES:     Somebody told me recently that he
              thought the wine tasted like beetroot.

ALCIBIADES:   Well, that is, I believe one of the compar-
              isons commonly used by the tasters of
              wine.

SOCRATES:     But then somebody else, who agreed with
              him about the beetroot, said that it
              tasted sweet and acid, too.

ALCIBIADES:   Like pickled beetroot.

SOCRATES:     Exactly.

ALCIBIADES:   So what's your problem?

SOCRATES:     I realised immediately that this is one of
              the ways that we have of talking about

flavour. It is the way of analogy: we say that something tastes like something else. The next level of sophistication is abstraction: instead of saying that oranges taste a bit like honey, we identify an abstract quality, sweetness, which they have in common with honey. Would you agree?

ALCIBIADES: I would.

SOCRATES: And would you also agree that abstraction involves putting our multifarious experiences of the world into little jars labelled 'sweet', 'red', 'rough', and so on?

ALCIBIADES: Of course.

SOCRATES: The question is, then, when it comes to flavour, how many jars should there be?

ALCIBIADES: I believe that wise men have commonly said that there are four.

SOCRATES: And what are the labels on these jars?

ALCIBIADES: They read: 'sweet', 'salty', 'sour' and 'bitter'.

SOCRATES: Why these four?

ALCIBIADES: Because these are the four basic flavours. All others may be described in terms of these four or of combinations of them.

SOCRATES: And the flavour of, say, beetroot is not basic?

ALCIBIADES: Obviously not.

SOCRATES:    Why not?

ALCIBIADES:  Well, let us say that a basic flavour is a
valuable tool that helps us to survive.
Our ancestors—who knew nothing of
hunting, husbandry or agriculture—lived
on fruit. Now, fruit is sweet, so it is
important to be able to taste sweet things
in order to know that they are fruit. A
bitter taste is an indication that there
may be some poison present, and they
needed to be able to detect salt because
salt too is important to us.

SOCRATES:    And the sour taste? Lemons and limes
are fruits, too, but they taste very sour to
me.

ALCIBIADES:  I think I need time to think about that
one.

SOCRATES:    Don't trouble yourself, Alcibiades: you
have already shown that the number of
basic flavours must be at least three, and
perhaps four. Unfortunately, you haven't
shown me that it can't be greater than
four. Perhaps there are more than four
things that we need to know about
flavour in order to survive in the world.
What about the delightful flavours of
roast meat or of cooked mushrooms?
These seem to me to be similar in some

respect to each other, and they don't seem to be salty, bitter, sour or sweet. So perhaps they constitute a fifth flavour. And if five, why not six, or seven, or more?

ALCIBIADES: Ingenious physicians have discovered that to each of these four tastes there corresponds an area of the tongue that is so constructed as to be able to detect it.

SOCRATES: No doubt they have, Alcibiades, but perhaps there are areas of the tongue where other flavours are detected. Perhaps some parts of the tongue are adapted to the detection of more than one flavour. If your physicians are convinced that there are only four tastes, they may give up their research too soon.

ALCIBIADES: Look, Socrates, all this talk about food has made me very hungry so I really think I should be off now. So, yes, you've won: we can't know whether there are four basic flavours, or five, or more.

SOCRATES: But, Alcibiades, if you went away believing that, I wouldn't think I'd won at all.

ALCIBIADES: Oh, ye Gods. Why not, O Socrates?

SOCRATES: Because I do not think that we can talk

163

about taste and be certain that we know what we are talking about.

ALCIBIADES: Why the ... Why not, O Socrates?

SOCRATES: How can we tell that when other people use the word 'salt' they mean by the word what we mean by it?

ALCIBIADES: We give them a number of foods, some containing salt and some not, and we see whether they can accurately pick the foods with salt in them.

SOCRATES: Suppose we are dealing with people who know nothing of salt?

ALCIBIADES: Well, if they don't know anything about salt, then they're not going to talk about it, are they?

SOCRATES: But suppose their knowledge of salt is very limited. Suppose they live on the coast and the only salt of which they have knowledge is in the taste of sea water or the fish that come out of it.

ALCIBIADES: Then I suppose if we give them salt, they'll say it tastes like the sea.

SOCRATES: So they won't think of salt as we think of salt?

ALCIBIADES: No, their knowledge of salt will be more limited than ours, because they know only of the salty taste of the sea, whereas we know of salts which have been drawn from the sea or from inland springs and also of rock salt. If we introduce them to those kinds of salt of which we have knowledge, they will come to realise that what they know is just one kind of salt, a sub-category of the broader concept.

SOCRATES: But why should they think that?

ALCIBIADES: Because our knowledge of salt is more extensive than theirs (which, since we are Athenians and they are not, is hardly surprising).

SOCRATES: But why shouldn't we say that their knowledge of the flavours of the sea is more extensive than ours? Why should they talk of salt at all? Why shouldn't they just say that what we call the taste of salt is simply the taste of the sea, and that raw fish and seaweed share something of the same flavour?

ALCIBIADES: Because only the sea and things that come from it taste of the sea, whereas many things taste of salt.

SOCRATES: But our coastal dwellers will simply say that those things taste a bit like the sea.

ALCIBIADES: Then all this amounts to is that when we say something tastes of salt, they'll say it tastes like the sea. So the difference is purely one of language.

SOCRATES: Not at all. Their use of language tells us that they are dividing up the universe of flavour in a way very different to ours, because the sea tastes of many things other than salt. Take a raw oyster, for example ...

ALCIBIADES: Socrates, you know I can't take oysters. You know that when you saw me throw up after a plate of them you said it quite turned you off the whole idea of—

SOCRATES: I know what I said, Alcibiades.

ALCIBIADES: Anyway, I don't really see the point of this discussion.

SOCRATES: It has little application at present, but things may be different in the future. Perhaps we will forget how to cook. Perhaps there will be people who manufacture our food for us, so that all we have to do to make it fit to eat is to heat it up or even just to add water to it. Whatever we know of flavour will depend on these people's ingenuity. It will be in their interests to study the matter closely and to understand how we taste and what we taste.

ALCIBIADES: Philosophy I can take, Socrates, but not fairy stories. I'm off. God, I hope they're not serving shellfish.

# r is for revolution

Revolutionaries are simplifiers. The French in 1789 sought to replace the grotesque, Gothic complexities of feudal government with something more rational, more svelte. They even began to dress in a manner that befitted the austerity of republican government. So, less elegantly, did the Maoist Chinese during the Great Proletarian Cultural Revolution. The Filipino revolution of 1986 did little for sartorial standards but it did liberate Imelda Marcos' shoes. Imagine the complexity of a life lived among so many shoes: so many choices to make so many times a day, so much matching of the footwear to the garments, of both to the occasion. Better to cast them off and be shod in the plain, simple style of the people.

Simplicity is also the battle cry of the revolutionary in the kitchen. Simplicity, but never austerity: these people—chefs, restaurateurs, writers—have a living to earn, and they're not going to pay the mortgage by urging you to settle down to a nice plate of steamed rice or potato soup. The concept of simplicity which operates in their world is far from simple.

For example, take, if you can, *nouvelle cuisine*, the study of which offers an illuminating exercise for the student of gastronomic fashion. In its time, *nouvelle cuisine* was a culinary phenomenon that could equally represent both simplicity and excess. The devices seemed simple—when the food was on the plate, you could see an awful lot of plate—yet the ingredients were rare and the prices high.

Some found this paradoxical. Others, oblivious of the paradox and even of the potential for paradox, were merely confused. Malcolm Bradbury's novel *Cuts* is a nice, and very late, measure of public confusion on the matter. 'So it was,' says Bradbury, 'that summer of 1986, a time for purpose, for burnishing and cleansing, for doing away with far too much of this and a wasteful excess of that.' His first chapter is a litany of cuts both economic and personal. 'For they were cutting down flab by cutting out food,' he continues: 'that was the summer of jogging executives in Adidas sweatbands and of *cuisine minceur*, illustrated food, abstract sauceboat pictures without much content.' This is all very strange: *cuisine minceur*, an off-shoot of *nouvelle cuisine*, was indeed a matter of small amounts of artfully arranged food; and fair enough too, because it was a slimming diet, developed by Michel

Guérard for use in his fat farm, Les Prés d'Eugénie. Neither *nouvelle cuisine* nor *cuisine minceur* was very happening in 1986, and *cuisine minceur* had never really happened in any hands but those of M. Guérard. It's difficult not to suspect that Bradbury wanted to talk about *nouvelle cuisine* merely because it looked to him like an appropriately 1980s kind of a thing—style without content, minimalism at high cost—and that he chose to call it *cuisine minceur* because *minceur* sounded like an appropriately mean, pinched, kind of a word. In the face of these confusions, it's probably a good idea to be specific and to make it clear that *nouvelle cuisine* was a 1970s kind of a thing.

In October 1973, the readers of the *Nouveau Guide*, a French food magazine run by the restaurant critics Henri Gault and Christian Millau, were greeted by a cheery headline. '*Vive la Nouvelle Cuisine Française*' it said, and the accompanying article told of exciting developments in the restaurant world. There was a new generation of younger chefs—that's to say, chefs in their forties—among them Paul Bocuse, Jean and Pierre Troisgros, Roger Vergé, Michel Guérard; their work was innovative and exciting. And what they all had in common, said Gault and Millau, was an approach to food that could be summarised in ten points.

Ten is a good number, heavy with Biblical significance, and soon Gault and Millau's observations of what *was* happening were transformed by others into prescriptions of what *should be* happening. They became the ten commandments of *nouvelle cuisine*. First, said Gault and Millau, all these chefs rejected unnecessary complications. Second, they reduced the cooking times—and thus, it was said, brought out the true flavours—of fish and fowl, white meat and green vegetables. Third, they used only the freshest ingredients, buying daily at the market. Fourth, they shortened their menus, concentrating every day on only a few dishes, so as to ensure the highest standards. Fifth, they didn't hang or marinate their game. Sixth, they eliminated the traditional rich sauces, and especially the flour roux on which so many heavy sauces were based. Seventh, they sought inspiration from regional dishes rather than from the ponderous glories of Parisian *haute cuisine*. Eighth, they used new technology like microwaves and food processors. Ninth, they were mindful of their customers' health and steered clear of techniques like frying and of ingredients which were then thought to be undesirable, like animal fat. Finally, they were constantly inventive.

Gault and Millau's list is as interesting for what it leaves out as for what it includes. It says nothing about that essential revolutionary spectacle, the world turned upside down. In 1978, a French magazine noted that the new cooking involved giving entrées the names of puddings (like *sorbet de fromage de tête*) and puddings the name of entrées (like *soupe de figues*); it involved talking of fish as though it were meat (*rumsteak de sole*) and of vegetables as though they were cakes (*gâteau de carottes*).

More significantly, Gault and Millau say nothing about what the food looked like: 'You know, the big white plate with the purple and the crimson and the yellow blob, and three scallops arranged like the spokes of a wheel,' said the Melbourne food writer and former restaurateur Stephanie Alexander, when I asked her about the image of *nouvelle cuisine*. Stephanie came of age as chef and writer in the days of *nouvelle cuisine*; she knows perfectly well what it is that everybody associates with this style of cooking: the artful appearance of the food itself, thinly sliced, arranged flat on the plate in a geometric pattern like a painting. Like a Japanese painting, as often as not: the austere beauty of a plate of sashimi seemed to be the aesthetic ideal for many *nouvelle cuisine* chefs.

And it really was the chefs who were responsible for the appearance of what was served. Plating, as it's called, was done in the kitchen, and waiters—who in former times used often to dish up the food at the table from a serving dish—had little left to do but the fetching and carrying. Some argue that a decline in their professional standards was the result.

The idea of a *nouvelle cuisine* was anything but new. They were talking about it in Paris in the 1740s and, though whatever happened then has nothing to do with the recent use of the term, it should alert us to the fact that French cuisine has gone through several revolutions in its long history. As the historian and sociologist

Stephen Mennell points out, these revolutions all look rather similar: 'each ... involves (among other things) the pursuit of simplicity, the using of fewer ingredients with more discrimination, moving towards enhancing the "natural" flavour of principal ingredients, and in the process the production of a wider range of dishes more differentiated in flavour because less masked by the use of a common cocktail of spices, or the same basic sauces.' This might seem to imply that over the last two or three centuries, food in the West has been getting progressively simpler. Or, more plausibly, it might mean that the process of change is cyclical: after each of these revolutions, stagnation set in, the ideas of daring revolutionaries became dull orthodoxy until at length a new revolution was necessary to restore flavour and texture.

There's something to be said for this latter idea: the *nouvelle cuisine* of recent times was a reaction against the orthodoxy established in the early years of the century by Georges August Escoffier, but in his own time Escoffier too had been a revolutionary. The point is that in the hands of lesser men, in hotels and restaurants throughout the world, Escoffier's high cuisine had become a routine matter of rich sauces and expensive ingredients. This was the *ancien régime* that *nouvelle cuisine* sought to overthrow. And, sure enough, the cycle soon turned again: *nouvelle cuisine* came to be considered decadent, fussy, over-refined, exhausted. By 1987 the food writer and restaurateur Michael Symons could claim that, though *nouvelle cuisine* was the basis of the culinary style then dominant in Australia, the term itself was often considered unfashionable and was usually avoided.

Stephen Mennell does not, though, want to embrace the idea of cyclical patterns in changing taste. He seems to see each revolution not just as the overthrow of the reigning orthodoxy but as a renewal, a return to 'the same pursuit of refinement, simplicity, restraint ...' But the situation must be more complex than this: the pursuit may go on and the goals may be called by the same name, but can we be certain that they haven't subtly changed?

The trouble is that if the goals have changed, then the game might not always have been the same game. In confident days gone by, human history was written as a story of continual improvement, the thrilling account of our growth out of primitive simplicity into the rich, varied and above all complex life of the modern world. It was a consoling story. It wasn't true but it was consoling, and at least it was easy to write, because complexity is cumulative. It's much more difficult to write a story in which things get progressively simpler, which is perhaps why it's taken so long for cooking to get off the ground as a serious subject of historical inquiry. Historians of French food want to talk about things getting progressively simpler, but, really, things just can't have got progressively simpler: we started off gnawing berries and half-cooked mastodon bones, and how much simpler can you get than that?

In fact, historians like to begin their story of simplicity triumphant much later than this, in the seventeenth century. It was then, we're told, that La Varenne, master cook to the Marquis d'Uxelles and author of *Le Cuisinier françois*, swept away the Gothic elaborations of former times and introduced a new, rational simplicity. But then along came another master cook, known only as Marin, who in 1739 proposed to do away with the fabulous elaborations of the old style of cooking and replace it with something simple, cleaner and less complex. The great culinary revolutionary of the beginning of the next century was Antonin Carême, in one of whose meals an enthusiastic diner found 'every meat presented in its natural aroma—every vegetable in its own shade of verdure'. Then, at the beginning of our century, Georges August Escoffier appeared and, according to one of his modern admirers, 'cut down on the cumbersome garnishes that had survived from the eighteenth century' in order to serve up food that looked like food.

Bocuse in our own times, Escoffier seventy years before him and Carême at the beginning of the last century all sought simplicity, refinement and restraint, but we can have no warrant for supposing that Escoffier's idea of refinement was the same as Bocuse's or that Carême's idea of simplicity was the same as Escoffier's. In each case, the chef's notions of what food ought to taste like would have been formed by the chefs who came before him; it's a mistake to think that cooked food has some innocent, original flavour to which we can all aspire if our hearts are pure enough. You have only to read a recipe by any of these three great men to realise that if what they thought they were doing was simple, then the idea of simplicity with which we're dealing must be a socially constructed one. So what we have to ask is why a particular notion of simplicity should come into fashion at a particular time.

The proponents of *nouvelle cuisine* liked to depict the hour of its birth as a time of decadence and stagnation in which inventiveness was all but forbidden and every meal a depressingly familiar rearrangement of expensive ingredients: foie gras, truffles, caviar. So it might be that what happened was simply that the 1960s, era of fashionable rebellion, came knocking rather late at the kitchen door. But why was the door opened? Perhaps because behind it was a different sort of chef. The inventors of *nouvelle cuisine* were nobody's employees: they owned the kitchens in which they worked and were not bound by the rules and conventions of an international hotel. Perhaps this new freedom taught them the difference between spending money and earning it, and made them less keen on all those expensive ingredients.

This will come as a surprise to anybody who's ever seen the bill after an intimate little evening for two at Paul Bocuse's place. It may be true that the new dishes were more economical in that they took less time to prepare than what had gone before, but they were not likely to make less of a dent in the customer's bank balance. On the other hand—and perhaps this is the important point—they *looked* less expensive: there was less on the plate and, though it might be artistically arranged, it was never piled high to form an arrogant, luxurious, baroque edifice. We can see a parallel movement taking place in the world of fashion a few years after the birth of *nouvelle cuisine*. A black shirt by Comme des Garçons, fabulously expensive as shirts go, looks just like a black shirt. You have to feel the weight of the fabric to know you're getting value for money. Feel the weight of the fabric or, better still, read the label; owners of Comme garments know they've got big bucks on their backs and can usually find means of letting others know it as well.

This is why journalists are such essential auxiliaries to any industry dealing in luxury commodities: it can't have been coincidental that the rise of *nouvelle cuisine* was accompanied by a considerable growth in food journalism and photography. Now you could learn just by reading a newspaper, or even just by watching television, what an expensive dish looked like (and, of course, *nouvelle cuisine* always photographed very prettily). 'Suddenly food was the star,' says Stephanie Alexander, 'and anything and everything to do with anyone's experience of eating out in the restaurants of the *nouvelle cuisine* chefs was top news.' Besides, the good thing about eating in restaurants is that it's really easy to let others know how much you're spending. The menu without prices, specially reserved for guests, is happily a thing of the past.

We don't just buy what we're told to buy, but we do desire what we're told is desirable. It's easy to blame the fickleness of our desires on those who tell us what we're supposed to want, the critics and the journalists. But though these are indeed dangerous allies for a chef to have, they are just one side of a triangle of exploitation and dependency that also involves producers and consumers. The writers need something new to write about and consumers, having been taught to expect novelty and inventiveness, expect it all the time.

This was the undoing of *nouvelle cuisine.* Soon, the sight of a fillet of chicken breast, thinly sliced, fanned out like a deck of cards and placed over—always over, never under—a delicate sauce on a black octagonal plate became just plain boring. The talent for innovation which *nouvelle cuisine* demanded of its practitioners was too much for the second-rate, who instead offered novelty in the form of perverse combinations. Meat and fish were cooked with Pernod or with raspberry vinegar and with all manner of fruit: strawberries, mangoes and, of course, Chinese gooseberries, which, having changed their name to kiwi fruit, became almost inescapable in the 1980s. There wasn't a single course on the menu where you could be sure you were safe from kiwi fruit.

What had once looked simple now looked baroque and complicated. French chefs turned increasingly to those peasant origins which every French chef is supposed to have. Food became rich, gutsy, comforting. It was, we were told, '*la cuisine de grande mere*', 'granny food'. By the mid-1980s, the English food writer Paul Levy was applauding the return of mashed potato (this, though, was potato mashed very creamily by the Parisian chef Joël Robuchon) and congratulating some Californian chefs for a dish that, in defiance of the picturesque and two-dimensional practices of *nouvelle cuisine*, actually stood up from the plate.

Were we back, then, on the road to simplicity and refinement? It ought to be apparent by now that the question does not have much meaning. There's an obvious sense in which the stews and soups and cassoulets that *grande mere* used to make are both coarser and more complex than the purees and terrines of *nouvelle cuisine*. There's another and equally obvious sense in which they're simpler and more refined: the ingredients are less extravagant, the processes less elaborate, the judgements required less minute.

But we're not really comparing wholesome peasant food with the frigid pleasures of the restaurant table; what we're really comparing are two sorts of restaurant cuisine. On the one hand, we have cuisine that claims inspiration from, among other things, the food of Japan; on the other we have a cuisine that claims inspiration from, among other things, the sort of food that French peasants might occasionally have eaten when they were lucky enough. The line of descent did not pass from Carême through Escoffier and Bocuse to Joël Robuchon's granny. All these grannies are polite fictions, created out of the urgent need to find a cuisine that, whatever else it might be, is not *nouvelle cuisine*.

The point, however, was not just to refrain from being *nouvelle cuisine* but at least to be a cuisine of some kind or other. In the wake of *l'année 73*, French chefs looked to their grannies because what they feared, now that the *ancien régime* had been overthrown, was a sort of anarchistic self-expression unconnected with culinary tradition. This was what Damien Pignolet, an Australian chef of pronounced Gallic affections, saw when he looked at what the revolution had wrought in Australia. 'It has no allegiance,' he said of what was cooked by the children of the revolution. 'It has no passion other than the passion of its creator.'

A kinder view is that *nouvelle cuisine* was a bit like adolescence: at times it could be hell, and you wouldn't want to do it again, but it's a stage you just had to go through. Stephanie Alexander still remembers the feeling of liberation amidst all the excesses. 'I wanted to use salads more, I wanted to minimise the number of distractions on a plate,' she told me. 'I was prepared to look at combining food in a way that I hadn't before.' Damien Pignolet agrees that *nouvelle cuisine* usefully encouraged people to think more laterally about food, but he's worried that it has left us a generation of cooks who don't understand the use of fat and salt: 'Try to cook something in water, without salt, and expect it to express some dignity of flavour—forget it.' This, alas, is so often the legacy left to us by the terrible simplifiers of revolution: a bland Generation X with more freedom than they know what to do with.

# S is for saunders

Towards the end of the fifteenth century, a social-climbing fellow of Merton College in the University of Oxford decided to exchange his surname for a more interesting one. So he took to himself the new and stylish cognomen 'Saunders'. The name which he abandoned as too commonplace was 'Shakspere'.

I mention this not to claim kinship with the Bard, or even with any medieval fellows of Oxford colleges, but for no other reason than to show that 'Saunders' is a name with resonance. It may fill an embarrassing number of double columns of grey type in all the telephone directories of the English-speaking world, but some people at least have thought it a name worth having. So nobody need fear that this chapter will be an essay in the fashionable discourse of self-reflexivity, or even—God forbid—an exercise in vanity. It is neither.

There is, as it happens, a dish called saunders.

The recipe appears in Eliza Acton's *Modern Cookery for Private Families*, first published in London in 1845. It's similar to shepherd's pie, only not quite as exciting:

> Spread on the dish in which the saunders are to be served, a layer of smoothly mashed potatoes, which have been seasoned with salt and mixed with about an ounce of butter to the pound. On these spread equally and thickly some underdressed beef or mutton minced and mixed with a little of the gravy that has run from the joint, or with a few spoonsful of any other; and season it with salt, pepper, and with a small quantity of nutmeg. Place evenly over this another layer of potatoes, and send the dish to a moderate oven for half an hour.

This is all expressed with the economy that makes Eliza Acton one of the finest writers of recipes in the English language. Only the somewhat antique phrase 'underdressed beef' needs to be explained. In this context, dressing beef simply means cooking it; there is no suggestion of adornment, which, given the dullness of the dish, there hardly could be.

Eliza Acton speaks of saunders as though the word were a plural, though presumably these saunders, plural or otherwise, have nothing to do with 'saunder', which is a shortened form of 'alexanders', the name of a herb also known as black lovage, black pot-herb and horse parsley.

By Eliza Acton's time, alexanders had given way in the English kitchen to celery. My surname also is a corruption of 'Alexander' and is generally supposed to be a medieval tribute to the unruly Macedonian youth of that name. The name of the herb, which was known to the Greeks and the Romans, may be another tribute. It is possible, I suppose, that my name derives from that of the herb, and, frankly, I'm not sure which is worse, to be named after a murderous social upstart or a bunch of shiny green leaves that everybody lost interest in sometime before the Battle of Trafalgar.

*The Oxford English Dictionary* is unhelpful on the subject of saunders. It asserts that the name is a variation of 'sanders' (we Saunders are accustomed to this sort of indignity) but the earliest reference it gives for sanders is from *A New System of Cookery*, published only eighteen years before Eliza Acton's book. What, alas, seems certain, though, is that all we have here is a way of doing up some leftovers. Shepherd's pie and cottage pie, which it closely resembles, are extravagant by comparison—there are onions in cottage pie and perhaps even Worcestershire sauce—but they too belong to the same frugal tradition. 'A recipe for the tough cuts of meat that were likely to come the way of the cottager or farm labourer,' says Elisabeth Luard of cottage pie in her *European Peasant Cookery*. 'Equally useful for any bits which might be left over from the Sunday joint.' Shepherd's pie—which, of course, always uses mutton rather than beef—is, she says, 'much favoured by the shepherd wives of Cumberland and the Lake District, mincing being a particularly good trick for tenderizing tough mutton'. (*Is* much favoured or *was* much favoured? Some of Ms Luard's sentences are verb-free, so I can't say whether these thrifty practices still persist amongst pastoral workers in the north of England. Do they still eat sheep? Their own sheep? Or do they heat up frozen lamb curries in the microwave?)

Of course, the economical use of leftovers is an essential part of good cooking the world over. The tragedy of English cuisine is that its most prudent habits have been taken as characteristic of the whole—rather as though your sartorial standards were to be judged by the old pair of stained Levis that you wear for painting the front of the house—and the real tragedy is that nobody has been more guilty of this misapprehension than the English themselves.

Too often, prudence has mouldered into meanness, and meanness, like a damp stain, has spread out from the realm of household economy to discolour a whole attitude to what is eaten. Mean people can't afford—or think they can't afford—to be picky about their food, but in England this hasn't stopped them recoiling in disdain from so many foods that are plentiful and cheap: offal, of course (of *course*), but also fungi and small birds. (Was it the same spirit—a legacy of Empire—that for so long prevented urban Australians from eating kangaroo? Is it what still stops them eating horse?)

One could argue that there's a certain proud austerity in an inhibited, conservative palate and an unwillingness to spend much on food; think what a Japanese monk, with no money and little freedom of choice, might do with the ingredients immediately to hand in the monastery garden. Unfortunately, in England meanness of spirit and meanness with money usually come together with meanness of effort. The English don't go to enough trouble.

It was not always so. Looking back on rural life in the 1880s, Flora Thompson describes how two days and two nights would be devoted to the making of calf's foot jelly; but, she adds, in those days cookery was looked upon as an art, and few would want to take such trouble nowadays. She was writing in 1945, at around which period Jane Grigson, a very fine food writer indeed, was still serving her time amidst the horrors of boarding school rice pudding. Only many years later, and in France, did Jane Grigson discover that rice pudding could be perfectly agreeable if made slowly, flavoured with a vanilla pod or cinnamon stick and eaten with lots of double cream. 'Like so many other English dishes,' she writes, 'it has been wrecked by meanness and lack of thought.'

This is nicely put, because, of these two negativities, lack of thought is as significant as meanness. It's one thing to be mean—too mean with money to pay for a vanilla pod, too mean in spirit to think of double cream as anything but an outrageous indulgence—it's quite another to be so unthinking as to be unable even to conceive that such things might be part of the dish. The people who fed the young Jane Grigson may or may not have thought time and trouble appropriate investments in the preparation of certain foods—I suspect they thought no food worth the effort—but I'm sure they simply couldn't imagine that, of all things, rice pudding might be worth it. For them, time and trouble meant elaborate, complex dishes.

If that's your view of food, then there are two ways you can go. You can decide that good food is complicated and expensive (a prevalent English misconception) or you can decide that the skills of the kitchen are good for nothing but the production of elaborate and complex dishes, and are therefore unnecessary in a nation endowed with the finest primary produce. The latter seems often to have been the view of the Victorians; when it came to domestic cuisine, what they called 'made-up' dishes—stews, say, or ragouts—enjoyed low prestige because they were suspected of being cunning, foreign tricks for disguising poor ingredients. Stout-hearted English ingredients were not afraid to appear unadorned on the table, roasted or boiled.

By the time Victoria came to the throne, this fondness for plain food had often been remarked upon, even by people like Grimod de La Reynière who had never sat at an English table. Writing at the beginning of the nineteenth century, Grimod referred to the English as 'these arrogant and greedy islanders, who persecute, destroy and despise all the other nations of Europe' (which was a bit rich coming from a compatriot of Napoleon Bonaparte). He thought it remarkable that so proud a nation could manage nothing in the culinary line beyond turtle ragout, beef steak, pudding and chicken boiled in water.

Of course, one expects this sort of thing from the French, but when the Scandinavians start talking like this, the time has come to ask yourself or your cook a few searching questions. 'The art of cooking as practised by most Englishmen does not extend much beyond roast beef and plum pudding,' wrote a Swedish visitor to England in 1748, thus giving a clear indication that the people of whom he wrote were in severe trouble.

The ultimate expression of this English love of commodities uncontaminated by art was the meal that consisted of scarcely more than a single ingredient—goose, turtle, turbot, whitebait, salmon—offered in copious quantities and with little in the way of side dishes, sauces, or culinary skill to distract the diner's attention. There was nothing here to foster imagination or dexterity in English cooks, and the result was what one writer calls the 'decapitation' of English cookery. This is perhaps not exactly the right word: the profession of cooks in England still had a head but it was no longer an English head. At the top were foreigners, imported from France and cooking in a French style. Whether admired or resented, their activities could do nothing to provide domestic cooks with standards to which they could aspire. This lack of native models working at the highest level of culinary achievement has resulted, as Jane Grigson observes, in a lack of professionalism in the English kitchen.

Attempts to ape the French were at first not admired. In 1862, Captain Gronow, a man-about-town in London and Paris for nearly half a century and an officer of the Guards at Waterloo, remarked that the nation of Shakespeare and Milton could boast 'not one single masculine genius in the kitchen'. Clearly, he had enjoyed the plain English dinners of his youth—the Mulligatawny and turtle soups, the salmons and turbots, the saddles of mutton, the roast beef, the fowls and tongue and ham, the 'universally-adored and ever-popular boiled potato'—though he observed that English vegetables, 'the best in the world', were never favoured with a sauce and usually came to the table cold. This solid fare was sometimes accompanied, he said, by a few timid and unsuccessful attempts at continental cookery. They were contemptible and nobody touched them.

The trouble was that English cooks didn't understand what the French were up to. They thought the French were doing the same thing as them but charging more for doing it. They did not understand that this great array of sauces, stocks, coulis, roux, glazes and demi-glazes, made by the laborious reduction of expensive ingredients, was not a foppish embellishment of good cooking;

it was what good cooking was now all about. These reductions were the *fonds*, the foundations, of a style of cooking that was a matter of delicate mixtures and infusions of flavour. England was stuck (and to some extent is still stuck) in a medieval world of puddings and pies, roast meats, boiled meats and violent contrasts of flavour.

What had happened was that the highest French cuisine had entered its classical era. There were established ways of doing things, there were prohibitions, there was subtlety, there was restraint; and now the English cook was excluded from the colonnades of *haute cuisine* unless he could demonstrate some mastery of the French way of doing things (female cooks were, of course, totally excluded anyway). Your opinion on whether or not this was a bad thing may well depend on how you feel about roast lamb with mint sauce. The pleasures of this dish, one of the simple glories of the English kitchen, are largely incomprehensible to the French because it offers a contrast of flavours too stark for the classical palate (though, come the beginning of the twentieth century, mint sauce, along with cranberry, horseradish and several others, was officially admitted into the French canon by the great Escoffier).

There are advantages and disadvantages here. On the one hand, perhaps it is this medieval willingness to countenance such combinations of sweet and savoury that has made the English palate more receptive than the French to Indian and Chinese food. On the other hand, the

English palate has not only inherited a medieval fondness for meat above all other things, but it has bequeathed this unhealthy taste to America and Australia.

In the year 1508, the anonymous author of the *Boke of Kervynge* warned his readers to beware of green salads and raw fruit if they valued their health. The warning seems to have been unnecessary: the English were not much interested in vegetables and were to remain uninterested over the next few hundred years. At the beginning of the nineteenth century, even the more expensive English private schools were guilty of not giving their young charges very much in the way of vegetables. Some students are reported to have suffered from scurvy, and it is not for nothing that the English are a notoriously constipated nation, much obsessed with their bowels.

When the English did turn their attention to vegetables, they seem to have done so firmly convinced that the result would be unremittingly dull. They were seldom disappointed, and there was little danger that anything like enjoyment would tempt them to repeat the experience in a hurry. In the middle of the last century, a certain Janey Ellice set down her recipe for a boiled salad. It begins without much promise—'Take Beetroot. Boil it well and slice it neatly.'—and continues with even less: 'Take Celery. Boil it well and cut it in large pieces.' It recommends adding to this some slices of boiled potato and perhaps Brussels sprouts together with a 'rich Salad Sauce composed of cream, Eggs and mustard'.

Complaints about the poor quality of English salads stretch over four hundred years, from Giacomo Castelvetro in the early seventeenth century to an English writer of our own day who recently issued a comprehensive anathema on his compatriots, their ignorance of lettuce, their meanness with olive oil, their fearful insistence on washing everything in copious amounts of water. No wonder Philip Muskett—condemned to life in colonial Sydney, surrounded by the best produce in the world and the worst cooks—looked so longingly to France, where 'to the great body of people ... life is more pleasant than to the rest of humanity', and where they knew how to make a decent salad.

There's something both funny and sadly familiar about Muskett's laborious comparison of the French and the English salad. The English, he explains, quarter their lettuce, leave it to soak in water for some time and then put it on a plate to drain, thus efficiently rendering it damp while leaving undisturbed whatever minute insects it might contain. Next, they cut it into fine shreds and add some slices of hard-boiled egg, after which 'a mysterious mixture known as salad-dressing' is poured over the whole sorry mess: 'Thus is produced the orthodox English salad, which everyone, probably from patriotic motives, pronounces to be extremely nice.'

Muskett's compatriots had inherited their British forebears' pride in animal husbandry. The English of his day thought very highly indeed of their meat: fat sheep and cattle, the ponderous result of two centuries of selective breeding, fed on a carefully calculated diet of turnips and other vegetables, with oats and barley, linseed and oilcake. Their cousins in New South Wales regarded 'lean' as a term of disapprobation when applied to meat, and in the early days of the colony they'd had to be bullied by the governor into growing vegetables.

Not only were there few vegetables on the Australian plate, but those that were there were chosen from a narrow range. Philip Muskett noted that seed and plant catalogues regularly contained many more vegetables than his countrymen seemed to want. They were advertised—globe artichokes, Jerusalem artichokes, asparagus, cardoons, celeriac, eggplant, kohlrabi, salsify, sea kale, sweet corn—but nobody bought them. (Surprisingly, he also lists the unromantic Brussels sprout among the neglected vegetables and recommends it for 'all the cooler parts of Australia'.) Would Australia ever produce such salads as the French enjoyed? Muskett took comfort from history: little regarded when first introduced to Europe, the tomato looked for a time like a complete non-starter, yet now it was universally loved. Perhaps in Australia the eggplant, the asparagus and all the rest would follow the same slow path to recognition.

But one can hardly blame Muskett's contemporaries for seeking in Australia what so many of them couldn't have enjoyed in the old country. The nineteenth century was a time of grinding poverty in rural England, but at least farm labourers could grow their own vegetables; in the towns, people lived on bread, potatoes and cup after cup of hot, strong tea, which allowed them a delusion of warmth and comfort. It's hardly surprising that those of them who were lucky enough to make it to Australia should have revelled in the prospect of meat three times a day.

They retained their love of tea, though, and it's worth remarking how unusual is this English enthusiasm. By the nineteenth century, we find a whole population, from the highest to the lowest, devoted to a couple of imported products. They had to buy them, of course. They couldn't grow their own tea and sugar: this could only be done, far away, by those dark-skinned races who laboured under the benevolence of British rule. So, in many respects, a cup of hot, sweet tea is a sort of symbol of all that has been wrong with English cooking: it's easy to prepare and it comes from somewhere else.

Eliza Acton didn't write for those who drank tea because they knew no better or could afford no better. Her book is a friendly but stern school of culinary skill. The chapter on beef, which ends with bargain-basement dishes like saunders, begins with a good example of her methods: a recipe for beef steak *à la française*. The reader is told to season the steaks, dredge them with flour and fry them in butter. She (for English cookery writers of Eliza Acton's vintage address themselves to female cooks or to the women of the house who supervise their work) is then told to turn to another chapter for the recipe for olive sauce. Here it emerges that the olives require dexterous handling: 'Remove the stones from some fine French or Italian olives by paring the fruit close to them round and round in the form of a corkscrew: they will then resume their original shape when done.' After weighing the olives, blanching them in boiling water, draining them and leaving them in cold water for up to an hour ('proportioning the time to their saltiness'), the cook is to stew them in a pint of rich brown gravy or *espagnole*. This means turning to the previous chapter, devoted to gravies, which explains how to take eschalots, carrots and ham, together with a number of spices, and turn them into an *espagnole* by stirring them in butter over a moderate fire for twenty minutes, gradually adding a strong veal stock, stewing it all for half an hour or more and skimming. The dish is but a single entrée—to be accompanied, perhaps, by soup and lobster *au béchamel*, and followed by haunch of venison and an array of vegetables—yet there can be no doubt of the time and trouble necessary for its preparation. At the time she wrote, Eliza Acton's work was soon to be superseded by that of more commercial writers like Isabella Beeton, who wrote for a busier, less devoted readership. Yet she surely shows the way that English cookery could have gone with her patience, her professionalism, her respect for culinary skill, and, of course, her pronounced Francophilia.

# t is for table talk

There is a large and ornate ballroom in one of Sydney's better known hotels. Like most such rooms in many such places, it's ornate in an antique sort of way recalling the stifling splendours of the *deuxieme empire*, the age of gilt and gelt, Rothschilds, Escoffier, César Ritz and Edward VII. There I sat one evening in spring, a guest of the wine industry, least distinguished of about eighty diners.

The table arrangement was cruciform and I was seated in one of the armpits of the cross, so there was nobody on my right. There was somebody opposite me, but we were separated by a table decoration of tropical luxuriance and an expanse of white linen so wide you could have landed a jumbo jet on it. There was nothing to do, then, but talk to the man on my left. He had obviously come in a job lot with the rest of the furnishings: you got so many ormolu picture frames, so many red velvet curtains, so many imitation Louis-the-something-or-other chairs, and so many tubby, bearded men with bow ties and cummerbunds who looked as though they ought to be drinking pink champagne from a can-can dancer's slipper.

We talked a lot, the tubby, bearded man and I, about wine, restaurants and how much he was enjoying the meal. He was strong on autobiography, conscientious as to detail, deaf to irony, and easily one of the most boring people I have ever met. What made the experience particularly hideous, though, was the way in which he managed not only to bore me but at the same time to give me the impression that I was boring him. It doesn't matter that he could, no doubt, have truthfully said the same thing about me. All that matters is that, for many courses, he and I were bound together in a hideous mutual embrace of tedium. It was *Huit Clos*. I have been to several such events since, but I haven't seen him again.

It's easy to forget that this sort of experience is an amenity largely unique to modern industrial civilisation. In tribal communities and peasant villages, the people who bore you over dinner are, for the most part, the people who've been boring you all your life. New bores and the challenge of conversation with a stranger are things to be dealt with only in a mobile or an urban society. When Brillat-Savarin set down his requirements for a good dinner party, what he said reflected not only the tastes of Paris in the early nineteenth century but also its growing social possibilities. 'Let the number of guests be no more than twelve, so that the conversation may always remain general,' he said. 'Let them be so chosen that their professions will be varied, their tastes analogous, and that there be such points of contact that the odious formality of introductions will not be needed.'

Wisely, perhaps, Brillat-Savarin doesn't report what the conversation was like at these dinners, but others from around the same time do try to tell us what was said over the Dresden or the Spode. They are people with good memories, or a talent for shorthand, or a tendency to have to leave the room every few minutes, notebook in pocket, to answer what they probably referred to as a call of nature. Or perhaps they just made it up. Sometimes, though, a particularly acute reporter (or a particularly fine writer of fiction posing as a particularly acute reporter) can make us believe that we really can know what the talk sounded like.

Here's a brilliant and beguiling example. It's suspiciously clear and we can be quite specific about it and where it comes from. It comes from Wednesday, May 15, 1776, the day when Dr Samuel Johnson met John Wilkes. Johnson's friend and biographer James Boswell recounts the story and he does so with a good deal of self-satisfaction; reasonably enough, because it was certainly a triumph to bring them together. Johnson and Wilkes were unlikely to get on well or even to want to meet each other: Johnson was a Tory and a moralist, Wilkes a political radical and a sexual libertine; they had attacked each other in print. So Boswell, with the psychological acumen that helped to make him a good biographer, did it by trickery.

'Mr Dilly, Sir, sends his respectful compliments to you,' he said to Johnson, 'and would be happy if you would do him the honour to dine with him on Wednesday next along with me . . .' When Johnson said that he would come, Boswell added that he assumed Johnson would do so only if the company was likely to be agreeable to him.

'What do you take me for?' said Johnson. 'Do you think I am so ignorant of the world, as to imagine I am to prescribe to a gentleman what company he is to have at his table?'

Well, Boswell replied, he was really only trying to protect his friend from company that he might not enjoy. The company might be very uncongenial to him: even John Wilkes might be there.

Johnson was indignant: 'And if Jack Wilkes should be there, what is that to *me*, Sir? . . . I am sorry to be angry with you; but really it is treating me strangely to talk to me as if I could not meet any company whatever, occasionally.'

On the appointed day, the two of them met in their friend Dilly's drawing room, where Johnson caught sight of the despised Wilkes and could hardly restrain himself. But then the cry of 'Dinner is upon the table' summoned them all in and they sat down without any show of bad humour. Wilkes placed himself next to Johnson and, says Boswell, began to work upon him the charm for which he was famous:

> No man ate more heartily than Johnson, or loved better what was nice and delicate. Mr Wilkes was very assiduous in helping him to some fine veal. 'Pray give me some leave, Sir:—It is better here—A little of the brown—Some fat, Sir—A little of the stuffing—Some gravy—Let me have the pleasure of giving you some butter—Allow me to recommend a squeeze of this orange—or the lemon, perhaps, may have more zest.'
>
> 'Sir, Sir, I am obliged to you, Sir,' cried Johnson, bowing, and turning his head to him with a look of 'surly virtue', but, in a short while of complacency.

This is such an appealing snapshot—it seems to bring us so close to real people sitting down to a real dinner more than two hundred years ago—that it's easy to forget that what we have here is a literary artefact. No doubt Samuel Johnson and John Wilkes did dine together one spring day in 1776, but between us and that event stand not just two centuries, not just Boswell's memory (which, good though it may have been, was human and fallible) but also Boswell's desire as biographer to present his hero in a flattering and surprising light. So to get the best out of Boswell, we have to look not only at what he tells us but also at what he takes for granted.

He takes it for granted that people may have friends who differ very widely from each other in political opinions and he takes it for granted that one may be a guest at a friend's table without knowing who one will meet there. He takes it for granted that one may perhaps meet one's political enemies there and, finally, he takes it for granted that the rules of what Johnson calls 'the world' oblige one not only to be polite under these circumstances, but to be so polite as to allow the possibility of being won over by the charm of the enemy.

For Boswell, the table is a particular sort of arena: an arena for conversation—animated, perhaps, but always polite—among people who may be strangers to each other. He is describing a very sophisticated society, one in which political conflict has been so restrained and civilised as not to disrupt dinner. On the other hand, nothing here is stiff or formal: this isn't the sort of feast or banquet at which everybody has to be quietly attentive to a speech, a song, a poem or a floor show.

So perhaps there are two kinds of table: the table at which talk is highly formalised and the table at which it isn't. This is not a very hard and fast distinction, but at least we can imagine what the two kinds of table sound like in their most extreme incarnations: at the most formal table, only one of those present is speaking; at the least formal, half of those present may at any one time be speaking. Of course, if more than half are speaking then there's probably somebody who isn't listening, which means that some at least of the social restraints have failed. This is a failure which the less formalised table courts and which the formalised table tries to escape only at the cost of imposing a rather rigid structure on events.

But there is another kind of table: the table where nobody's saying anything. The most obvious reason for silence is that there's nobody to talk to, but even the solitary diner may nonetheless be a performer in a kind of social arena; there may be reasons for eating alone other than the lack of suitable company. At the *Daijosai* or Great Food Offering, which precedes the enthronement of the Emperor of Japan, the new monarch eats rice by candlelight accompanied only by two female attendants. The ceremonial nature of the occasion certainly qualifies this table as an arena, though perhaps we shouldn't speak of the new Emperor as dining alone, since he is in fact sharing his rice with the Sun Goddess.

But even if the Sun Goddess hasn't been invited, the solitary diner may have good reasons for eating alone. The anthropologist Nigel Barley reports that the Dowayo people of the Cameroons consider it impolite to watch strangers eating. This was good news for Barley, who hated Dowayo cooking and was able to retire to his hut with the food they'd given him and refrain from eating it without giving offence.

Even a table at which two or more people are seated may still be a silent one. Perhaps they don't get on with each other, perhaps they're not very happy, or perhaps they're silent because good manners demand it. The special house or room in which the Japanese tea ceremony takes place is without doubt a social arena—what goes on there is governed by extensive rules of etiquette—but it is also a sanctuary from the world, where, as one writer tells us, 'one can consecrate himself to undisturbed adoration of the beautiful'. The ritual itself begins in silence. Similarly, the meals shared by women in the United Arab Emirates are arenas of elaborate social ritual—the hostess, ritually modest about the feast she has laid on, ritually encourages the guests to greater consumption and the guests ritually praise the lavish nature of the meal—but they are not arenas for conversation: out of respect for the food, the meal proceeds for the most part in silence. Both these silences, the Japanese silence and the Arab silence, are insisted upon so that the attention of the participants in the meal or ceremony may be directed elsewhere than towards each other: to the beauty of their surroundings or of the occasion or to the food with which God has provided them.

On the whole, this sort of behaviour has seldom gone down well in the Christian West. To be silent is to be a boor, and to be silent because you're concentrating on your food is to be a boor with quite the wrong priorities. 'If dolts think that it is a great virtue to say nothing at table,' said a French writer of the sixteenth century, 'pigs and other such beasts would by their lights be equivalent to the most noble people.' There are exceptions to this rule of enforced conviviality, notably Christian monks, who are silent where the Rule of St Benedict holds sway. A monk is permitted to communicate with his brethren while they eat—he may ask for food to be passed to him—but he must do it in sign language, so that nobody's attention will be distracted from the voice of the brother who has been chosen to read to them all during their meal. The monk, unlike the Japanese tea drinkers and the Arab women, is being enjoined to direct his attention away from the fleshly pleasures of the food or the mundane reality of the refectory. This is not to say that the meal itself is unimportant. On the contrary, it is a ceremonial occasion, a communion among brothers who share their wine cups and help each other to food.

So all these silent meals, particularly the silent meals where more than one person is present, are silent in order that the attention may be concentrated. They are all, in one way or another, ritual or religious events, placing clear and obvious restraints on human behaviour.

But it's possible to restrain human behaviour without being quite so constraining. The ancient Greeks tried to do this at their *symposion* or drinks party (an event for which there is no real modern equivalent: it was not a cocktail party or a cheese and wine do but something that followed a meal).

The formal structure of the *symposion* was defined restrictively: the symposiasts were Greek, male and high-born. This last requirement kept out quite a lot of the Athenian population. In his comedy *The Wasps*, Aristophanes makes it clear that for a theatrical audience in the fourth century BC, the *symposion* was a foreign world of aristocratic licence. However, this licence was, at least in its early and more sober stages, quite strictly governed by rules of social usage. For example, though most of the symposiasts reclined on couches, there were rules as to who was allowed to recline and who was not. In the dialogue by Xenophon called *The Symposion*, Autolycus, being a minor, has to sit rather than recline beside his father Lycon. Indeed, this dialogue—though itself even more of a literary artefact than Boswell's account—seems to indicate that the *symposion* was not just a free-flowing conversation. Not long after the beginning of this party, a libation is poured, a paen is sung and a cabaret enters in the form of a girl who plays on the pipes, another who dances and an attractive boy who both dances and plays the lyre. Later on, there are more dancers, acrobats too, and the evening closes with a double-act featuring Dionysus, God of wine, inspiration and ecstasy, and his wife, Ariadne. Other accounts make it clear that the *symposion*, as a Dionysian ritual, was an arena for the delivery of poetry either specially written for the occasion or improvised on the spot. Even when the talking started, a strict rule of etiquette continued to hold sway. In Plato's *Symposion*, conversation, or rather the sequence of speeches, appears to move in an anti-clockwise direction around the room.

The Dionysian nature of the occasion was, perhaps, one reason why it should have been governed by elaborate rules; they served to regulate the consumption of alcohol and to maintain the symposiasts (at least at the beginning of the evening) in a moderate, good-humoured balance between the extremes of abstinence and drunkenness. A certain amount of sobriety was appropriate given that one of the purposes of the *symposion* was the education of adolescent boys (and not just their sexual education, though that as well). As in the public mess where Spartan men ate together, so in the Athenian *symposion* were the young men given an opportunity of questioning their elders: 'This,' says Xenophanes, 'is what you should say by the fire in the winter season, lying on a soft couch, full of food, drinking sweet wine and chewing chickpeas: "Who are you and from whence among men do you come? What are your years, noble Sir? How old were you when the Mede came?"' As conversational gambits go, these don't sound very ice-breaking, but, then, it was all very long ago and very far away.

A later Greek author, Plutarch, seems more urbane in his observation that the real trick at *symposia* is to talk philosophy without seeming to do so. All this, though, is the advice of insiders: Aristophanes—playing the outsider, though he very definitely wasn't one—suggests that the symposiasts' conversation consisted of name-dropping and big-noting themselves.

But both Xenophanes' advice and Aristophanes' satire

make it clear that these are the rituals of a small society. You may encounter strangers at the *symposion*, but the task of finding something in common with them is not going to be a demanding one.

To move from the world of the *symposion* to the sort of dinner that Boswell and Johnson enjoyed is to move from a small city, governed (in theory at least) on republican principles and founded upon a slave economy to a much larger city, the centre of a growing empire, and one of the birthplaces of capitalism. With a population of about three-quarters of a million, London in the middle of the eighteenth century was hardly a large city by modern standards. To contemporaries, though, it was almost unimaginably huge, larger than anything anybody had before encountered in Europe. But it wasn't just size that made London different: increasing trade brought with it new forms of social organisation, based no longer on the assumption that one's dealings would principally be with people that one knew well. What were needed now were a few stock phrases that could be used in a variety of situations and to a variety of interlocutors. It may well have been an intuition of these developments that led the author of *Gulliver's Travels* to publish in 1738 his *Complete Collection of Genteel and Ingenious Conversation, According to the Most Polite Mode and Method Now Used at Court, and in the Best Companies of England.*

Jonathan Swift reassures his reader that 'there is not one single witty Phrase in this whole Collection, which hath not received the Stamp and Approbation of at least one hundred Years . . .' Indeed, the whole thing is a string of colloquialisms, banalities, catch phrases and slang all threaded together with great skill into a set of three conversations. But, allowing for its cliché overload, Swift's book does perhaps give us some idea of the flavour of English conversation in the first half of the eighteenth century.

The second of Swift's conversations takes place at Lord and Lady Smart's house, where Lord Sparkish, Colonel Atwill, Mr Neverout, Miss Notable and Lady Answerall arrive as guests for dinner. They go in to eat just after three and, we're told, 'after the usual compliments' take their seats and begin with a few oysters. Some of the conversation is determined by the form of the meal: these people are not being treated (as we are when we sit down to dine) with a succession of courses. In Swift's day, everybody who could afford it dined *à la française*. This is why the talk at Lord and Lady Smart's table is punctuated by phrases like, 'Shall I help you to some Beef?', 'Pray, Mr. Neverout, will you please to send me a Piece of Tongue?', 'Miss, shall I send you some Cucumber?', and the very homely, 'they say, Fingers were made before Forks, and Hands before Knives'. All this suggests a certain degree of informality, as does the readiness with which they all shuffle up to make room for a late-comer, Sir John Linger.

Perhaps it's this informality that encourages them to

talk about the meal in front of them; the British upper classes hadn't yet developed their horror of talking about food. More generally, their conversation, despite its banality, can be decidedly robust: 'What; Mr. Neverout, you are in great haste,' says Miss Notable. 'I believe your Belly thinks your Throat's cut.' This, incidentally, reminds me of a story I have from a late nineteenth-century source of a great duchess of the eighteenth century turning round to the footman who was waiting on her at table and saying, 'I wish to God that you wouldn't keep rubbing your great greasy belly against the back of my chair.'

Presumably at most dinners conversation could be expected to become still more robust after the ladies had retired. Swift spares us the masculine profanities by cutting almost immediately to the third conversation, where the ladies are at tea. Had we stayed with the gentlemen, we might have been as shocked as François de la Rochefoucauld was in 1784. He enjoyed the frankness with which Englishmen discussed politics after dinner, but he also found their talk 'extremely free upon wholly undecent subjects', adding that very often he had 'heard things mentioned in good society which would be in the grossest taste in France'. In France, the ladies didn't retire: they stayed for the whole meal. (Though, come the nineteenth century, Lord Byron seems not to have wanted them to be there at all. He *said* that this was because he didn't like to see them eat—he preferred to think them above such unethereal vulgarity—but the truth seems to have been that he didn't like to see them being served first and getting the best parts of the chicken.)

Gross or not, what we see in these eighteenth-century English meals is an attempt to come to terms with a changing society, and a society that is similar to ours in recognisable respects: we too meet strangers at table; we too need to find common ground and means of address with them. And what, most of all, separates us—and Swift and Boswell and Johnson—from the volubility of the *symposion* and the silence of the monastery and of the tea ceremony is that we don't regard the meal as an instrument of moral education. The *symposion* is either a lesson or a seminary; the sort of meal at which Johnson met Wilkes may have been an education but really it existed for itself, for the pure pleasure of the food and the company.

We do, though, have meals for something other than pure pleasure: we have our working breakfasts, our working lunches, our working dinners. Fortunately for him, John Wilkes didn't have too much work on his hands. He had to determine that the lemon had more zest and he had to charm Johnson, but he didn't have to try to close a deal before dessert.

# U is for undead

Now is the moment for Death, lordly Death, to enter these pages. I wish I had a good wine with which to toast Him and placate His pride, but the fact is that I was drinking only a cheap Chardonnay spritzed with soda water when I heard a gentle rapping at my apartment door.

It was my neighbour and she was worried. Somebody had collapsed on the landing downstairs, she had sent for an ambulance, but would I come?

He was a man of middle age, balding, swarthy, wearing jeans, sitting on the floor with his back to the wall and his legs splayed. A bag of groceries lay next to him, not spilling any of its contents. I felt his neck for a pulse; there was none. I had never seen him before.

The ambulance men moved quickly, and their manner was brisk in a way that I had not anticipated. I don't know whether they had learned such sensitivity in the course of their work that they could tell immediately that the man on the landing was nobody to us or whether they were so insensitive that they just didn't care.

'Well, he's deceased,' said one of them with a cursory glance at the body. 'Look,' he added, helpfully, holding up a purpling dead hand, 'you can tell—the heart's not pumping the blood any more, so it's all fallen straight to the extremities.'

'A coronary?' I suggested brightly, getting into the spirit of the occasion (and voicing a fear never far from the heart of the professional food writer).

'Very probably, yes.'

The ambulance men busied themselves with phoning the police and setting up the electronic equipment that would confirm what we had all known the moment we first looked at the dead man. My neighbour and I closed our doors on the scene.

This was the closest I have ever been to a corpse (a human corpse, I had better add, since this a book about food) and I discovered a strange duality in the experience. As soon as I set eyes on him, I was struck by how unalive he looked, how untenanted, how like a man who wasn't going anywhere in a hurry. But, as I touched his neck—felt the ebbing warmth of his body, brushed my fingers against some bristles that had escaped his razor that morning—I had the curious feeling that at my touch he might spring suddenly to life.

The air of ambiguity that shrouds the newly dead is

my reason for writing here about the incident, because in the past, this ambiguity gave birth to legends: the dead, who seemed so nearly alive, separated from the living by the thinnest of veils, might walk amongst us, driven by strange appetites, fuelled by the most unholy nutriment.

'I shall cut off her head and fill her mouth with garlic, and I shall drive a stake through her body,' says Professor Van Helsing of Amsterdam when asked how he intends to deal with one of Count Dracula's victims. Bram Stoker (not always the most reliable guide to the undead) appears to have got this bit right: several cultures recommend putting garlic into the coffin or the grave of the suspected vampire. The Bulgarians used millet as well and, quite recently, the Romanians have used incense. Wine and bread can be useful, too; it was a Romanian practice to put them into the tomb, the idea being that if the vampire was supplied with a subterranean snack, it would not go seeking human flesh and blood. Another effective method is not to feed the creature but simply to keep it busy. Your typical vampire is an obsessive character and will count, very slowly, any grains you put into its grave. The Macedonians used millet, mustard seeds and oats; the Germans, linen and carrot seeds, whilst Slavic peoples used poppy seeds.

The vampire presupposed by these practices is obviously a sad, obsessive creature, far-removed from the suave, aristocratic seducer that we are used to. This is why the psychoanalytic idea of the vampire as a wish-fulfilment fantasy of power and sexual dominance seems more suited to the vampire of literature and the movies than to the vampire of folklore. The real vampire—the vampire that people have really believed in, and perhaps in some parts of the world still believe in—may have powers that are denied to the living, but it is far from omnipotent. On the contrary, it is confused, compulsive, driven only by hunger, and so hungry that even a few grains of millet or a little bread and wine will keep it occupied. These legends grew up among people who knew what hunger was; the vampire was the image of themselves in years when the harvest was particularly bad, aware of nothing but the gnawing in their bellies.

This, perhaps, is why the villagers of Romania regard werewolves and vampires with remarkable tolerance. According to the folklorist Harry A. Senn, they are looked upon as 'unorthodox but living members of the human community', and as such are to be treated with caution but not with utter loathing. (Senn pursued his researches among the villages of rural Romania in the late 1970s, which is why the present tense seems appropriate here, though back then the presence of a bloodsucker in the presidential palace may have been what was keeping belief alive.) Often, their hunger and thirst are under-standable enough: they want what the villagers want, the milk of domestic livestock.

Globally speaking, which, I wonder, is more common, the drinking of milk by adults or the eating of products made with animal blood? Outside of north America, northern Europe, Australasia and a few African tribes, most of the adult world is incapable of properly digesting milk: lactose—a sugar found in mammalian milk and almost nowhere else in nature—is indigestible unless broken down in the small bowel by the enzyme lactase, which in most ethnic groups disappears after the time of weaning. In general, I suppose, the herders of cattle are also consumers of blood, and many European peoples make blood puddings, sausages and cakes. The Masai of East Africa live on the milk of their herds and on their blood, which they draw from the living animal (this is also how the Mongol hordes lived off their own horses).

According to medical opinion fashionable in the America of 1911, this diet ought to keep them particularly healthy. A certain Dr Harlow Davis, a great advocate for fresh milk, observed with approval that the abattoirs of New York were visited every morning by consumptives in search of the freshest blood. 'To those persons who may think that the taste of the blood must be nauseating, I may add that with eyes closed it is practically impossible to tell the difference between the blood, and milk warm from the cow,' he said. 'Not only are they similar in taste, but likewise in physiological effects.' The idea that these two fluids are equally nourishing seems to bring us very close to the beliefs of those dairying people of Romania for whom the diet of the vampire and the werewolf were not very different from their own.

But, of course, the trouble with most vampires is that they do not restrict themselves to the milk, or even to the blood, of cattle: they seek human prey. If the garlic, the millet seed, the bread and the wine have failed to keep them in their place, which is six feet under, then it will be necessary to do what the Romanians do, or perhaps used to do: rub garlic on doors, windows and cattle. A similar method has been employed on the Philippines island of Bohol as a way of keeping off the local variety of vampire, a disconcerting creature called the *aswang*, which has the head of an animal, the body of a human and a protruding tongue about eight or ten feet long (though some of them are just half bodies with wings). *Aswangs* use their long tongues to search for small openings in bamboo houses and they prey on the blood of naughty children, pregnant women, the sick and the weak. However, potential victims can protect themselves by the use of garlic, smeared on as a sort of under-arm odorant.

The Romanian and Filipino customs make very obvious the main point about garlic: it's the smell that counts. A lot of witches, demons and the like are allergic to any strong odour but their own, which is why it is important to cut open the clove and smear on the garlic. When you cut garlic, you don't so much release the smell as create it by bringing a sulphur-containing compound into contact with an enzyme that converts it into something that in turn breaks down into pungent dalkyl disulfide. For this reason, I find it difficult to understand the practice of hanging garlic around the neck, though it certainly went on. The American folklorist Paul Barber writes of children forced to wear garlic garlands and of one poor girl who finally gave up, 'because no-one would play with her'. Perhaps the idea was that the power of garlic was such that the mere threat of it was enough to keep evil at bay.

A Romanian method for detecting the undead is to distribute garlic by the church door at Easter; anyone who doesn't eat is a vampire. Of course, this will work only in a garlic-eating culture, and I have to say that, suspicious as I am of people who won't touch the stuff, I rather like the idea of their being terrorised into it by the threat of a stake through the heart. However, we shouldn't suppose that the belief that there's something just a bit off about garlic is purely an Anglo-Saxon prejudice. It's true that in the seventeenth century John Evelyn thought that its 'intolerable Rankness' made it unsuitable 'for ladies' Palates' and that in the nineteenth century Isabella Beeton warned her readers that, 'The smell of this plant is generally considered offensive, and it is the most acrimonious of the whole alliaceous tribe.' But they could have cited the Latin poet Horace—who was very eloquent on the subject of garlic and what it did to the breath— or any number of other fastidious Romans, including Apicius, who didn't have much time for it in his cooking. The Romans were impressed, though, by the power of the herb. Pliny recommended its use against snakes, scorpions and various poisons, and dishes of garlic were left at the shrines of the witch-goddess Hecate.

But perhaps it's not the smell but the chemical which produces the smell that makes garlic so powerful a weapon against the undead. This is one of the implications of a well-known theory about vampires, propounded (how seriously I don't know) by Professor David Dolphin of the University of British Columbia. In 1985, Professor Dolphin proposed that vampires—that's to say those unfortunates who'd been accused of being vampires—might, in fact, have been victims of porphyria, an incurable and sometimes fatal genetic disease. He suggested that some of the symptoms of porphyria (pain, respiratory difficulties, skin lesions) could be relieved by an injection of heme, a component of haemoglobin found in red blood cells, bone marrow and the liver. So all those blood suckers were in fact trying to administer heme to themselves by drinking large quantities of blood. Other symptoms of vampirism, he said, are also symptoms of porphyria: having pointed teeth, for example, sensitivity to light and also sensitivity to garlic, because the dalkyl disulfide in garlic destroys heme.

This would certainly explain why no vampire would want to take the garlic at the church door—it might increase the severity of a porphyria attack—but, unfortunately, Professor Dolphin's hypothesis falls down on a number of counts. He doesn't seem to know enough about vampires and he doesn't seem to know enough about porphyria. Movie vampires may be highly sensitive to light, but Bram Stoker's Dracula isn't, neither are the vampires of folklore (some of them attack at noon) and traditional stories don't have anything to say about their teeth. As to porphyria: some forms of the disease are treated by *drawing* blood from the victim, and it's only the most extreme form, known as Gunther's disease, that's sometimes treated by blood transfusion. It has to be a transfusion, though: there's no evidence that heme can be absorbed through the gut and there's certainly no evidence that porphyria sufferers have a thirst for blood. If they don't have any such thirst, then the only thing that might send them in search of blood would be a belief that it would help relieve their condition, but no such belief can be found in any of the many communities around the world who've lived in fear of vampires.

Nor, incidentally, is there any evidence that porphyria sufferers are unable to eat garlic. So what is the role of garlic in the vampire myth and, for that matter, what is a vampire?

Belief in vampires is very widespread—it crops up all over the world—and there are lots of eyewitness accounts. But typically an eyewitness account will describe not the vampire at work, sucking blood, but the vampire at rest: lying in the grave, looking alarmingly alive and showing every sign of *having* sucked blood. It's always difficult to catch them in the act, and many of them are invisible: the body remains in the grave, the ghost roams the locality in search of victims. There tend to be a lot of victims, because vampirism occurs in epidemic form.

As to what really happens, Paul Barber suggests the following hypothesis. An epidemic disease, perhaps plague, hits the village; first one person dies, then lots of people. Vampirism is suspected and, reasonably enough, the authorities conclude that the person who died first must have been the accursed party. They open the grave and, sure enough, discover a corpse displaying all the symptoms of the undead: the limbs are pliant; the hair, the beard, the nails have continued to grow; the skin is not pallid but ruddy; there's blood, fresh blood, about the mouth. The authorities conclude that this is not a decomposing body, that it is still animated by some ghastly, evil parody of life.

But, in fact, these are the signs of death, not of life; of decomposition, not of vitality. After death, the body comes out of *rigor mortis*, so the limbs will become pliant again. The blood will have used up all its oxygen and so will have become darker, giving the corpse a ruddy, rather than a pallid appearance. Burying somebody face down was supposed to prevent that person from becoming a vampire, which is odd because it's a good way of inducing the symptoms of vampirism. As I know from the ambulance man, once the heart stops pumping, the movement of the blood is governed by gravity, so if you bury the deceased face down, blood will darken the cheeks and gather at the mouth. In any case, the gases of decomposition will force the blood up to the mouth and nostrils.

In fact, most bodies exhumed after a short while in the grave will look like vampires, which is why vampire hunters hardly ever failed to find what they were looking for. And when they wielded the stake, they drove the gases from the body and the vampire screamed as they were forced explosively past the glottis. As to the garlic: traditional medicine tends to be homoeopathic, you fight fire with fire, smell with smell. Which is why not only garlic, but also juniper, incenses and dung are useful against what looks like a smelly vampire but is in fact a putrefying corpse.

For us, a dead body is simply inanimate matter. It may change and move but its alterations have no more to do with what we call life than has the rusting of a kettle left out in the rain. For earlier cultures, however, a body that changed and moved was still in some sense alive. Barber mentions the distinction made in many cultures between those who have been long dead and those who have just died. The recently dead are dangerous. Unhappy in their new abode, they may try to leave or to get us to join them. Naturally, as the Romanians believe, those who have been wrenched suddenly from life are the most reluctant to let go.

Sometimes, I see dead people in my dreams, people I knew when they were alive. They walk around and talk, and when I ask them whether they are really dead, they say, yes, they are, but what difference does that make? Eventually, they learn what difference it makes, and their appearances become less frequent. I can understand their mistake, though, or rather my mistake. When I feel the stubble on my own warm chin, it seems almost natural that a man who died suddenly and alone, with a bag of groceries at his side, should want to rise up and go in search of the most basic of human needs: warmth, comfort and nourishment.

# V is for venery

As one of Martin Amis' characters observes, whatever you say after a first kiss will necessarily be cinematic. The same is true when you pour your first bottle of good wine at your first private dinner together. You can say something about the wine ('this is a rather interesting little chablis') or you can say something about the occasion ('I've been saving this wine for somebody really special') but anything you say is overwhelmingly likely to have been said before by many, many people, quite a few of whom will have been fictional characters in films, books or plays.

Nor will silence save you from cliché. Here's the same Martin Amis character—hornily adolescent Charles Highway, hero of *The Rachel Papers* and of my early manhood—wordlessly doing the honours, probably to the sound of late-middle-period Beatles: 'Now, as an opener, I decided to try something *rather* ambitious. I rose, poured our drinks, held her eye as we sipped, took her glass away. You really need to be six foot for this, but I gave it a go anyway ...'

*You*, by the way, are a man. I'm sorry, and I'd be very happy for things to be otherwise, but this seems to be one of those areas of heterosexual encounter where men are expected to be in command or to pretend to be. Taking her glass from her is a way of taking the initiative; showing off your knowledge of Burgundy or Bordeaux is another way of doing the same thing. (Which, presumably, is why Commander Bond always found it necessary to be such a bore about vintages.) There are women—I know there are, because I've met them—who taste wine with care, swish it around their mouths, smell corks and so on, but they do so (disappointingly) only because of their passion for wine, not because they're passionate about the person in front of whom they're displaying their passion for wine.

The man who takes command of the corkscrew is, of course, a banal avatar of that most banal of archetypes, man the hunter. It is an etymological coincidence but a happy fact that the same word, 'venery', means both the pursuit of game and the pursuit of sexual pleasure. Now, hunting (even that small subdivision of the activity that consists of hunting for sport) comes in many forms, from the undeniably decorative brutality of the Duke of Beaufort's hounds in full cry to the Australian practice of putting on plaid shirts and blasting away at ducks and conservationists. On this scale, setting dinner as a trap for your sexual quarry is somewhat on a level with falconry in the middle ages: it's all form, ceremony, fanfare and servants, without any certain hope of much blood at the end of the day.

Yet still we saddle up and ride forth. A Sydney restaurateur once told me that, come Valentine's Day, her establishment would be full of loving couples. An entire restaurant given over to serried ranks of candlelit tables for two and filled with lovesome murmurings—it must be an almost surreal or, more accurately, a Kafkaesque sight, recalling rows and rows of tiny desks, each with its brace of amorous clerks, clocking in every dawn for a day of routine smooching. But what are they after, these couples? Why go to a public place to eat with your loved one rather than staying at home and celebrating your passion in some more obvious way? Why are food and romance always such close companions?

One rather chemical explanation is that we've always had a touching faith in the ability of certain foods to stimulate desire. Casanova thought highly of alcohol (naturally), truffles, egg whites and oysters—oysters were particularly helpful, because you could drop one down the front of a dress and then chivalrously offer to retrieve it—but he recognised that the props and even the stage business are of less importance than the set. He knew that what really matters is ambience.

It's easy to forget that in his day this ambience was a

relatively new thing. For most of history, people didn't eat in couples: they ate in families or even larger groups in clearings, long huts or baronial halls. Sexuality, when it was represented at their tables, appeared in guises appropriate to the coarse sensibility of the crowd. Up to the sixteenth century, table decorations, known as 'subtleties', could sometimes take a form so unsubtle that one eighteenth-century writer could bring himself to mention them only in Latin: 'representations of the *membra virilia, pudendaque muliebria*, which were formed of *pastry*, or *sugar*, and placed before the guests ...' In other words, cocks and cunts: suitable tableware for the age of the codpiece, though today they might look a bit forward.

By the eighteenth century, wealth could buy privacy. It was the age of the intimate supper in the private room (perhaps even cooked by the host himself on a small table in the corner). Now a rich man like the French ambassador in Venice could employ a cook to prepare private meals for him and his mistress. In his case, the dishes, served in Sèvres porcelain, were left on a table in *bains maries* so that it was not necessary to have servants around disturbing the proceedings. The French ambassador in Venice, by the way, was a priest.

The following century was the age of the restaurant, so now you didn't have to be as rich as an ambassador to enjoy these intimate pleasures. You and the object of your affections could be served in a sumptuous private chamber like Room A at Kettner's in London, with its wallpaper of gold, brown and green, its gilt candelabra and its paintings of Italian landscapes. In England this was not quite proper—respectable women were seldom seen in restaurants—but in France and Austria they took a more relaxed view of these things: you could hire a really private room, one with no handle on the outside of the door. Or if you were a man you could ask Hugo, maitre d' at Maxim's in Paris, to find a woman for you with the aid of his little black book.

It is not difficult to see what the restaurant had going for it, perhaps still has going for it, as an aid to seduction. Invite somebody out to dinner and you're inviting that person to a public place—which sounds safe—but you're also proposing that together you perform what is really quite an intimate act. 'Eating and loving are perceived as such similar activities that we tend to talk of one in terms of the other,' says the anthropologist Jeremy MacClancy. 'We say we have lusty appetites, we hunger for love, feast our eyes, eat out our hearts, and suffer devouring passions.' In fact, compared to many societies ours is rather shy about the connection. MacClancy tells of the Mehinaku people of central Brazil, amongst whom the vagina is spoken of as the food of the penis. But they are not sexist, the Mehinaku: they also describe the penis as the food of the vagina, eaten in the act of intercourse by the female sexual mouth. It seems that Mehinaku men are often plagued by castration anxieties.

Other cultures go further, says MacClancy: many use

the same word for 'to eat' and 'to copulate'. Even if we don't go that far, some of us can come close. Back in the 1970s, a certain Alex Comfort brought out a grim little manual called *The Joy of Sex*. Subtitled 'a gourmet guide to lovemaking', it was divided like a meal into several courses: 'starters', 'main course', 'sauce and pickles'— which was where bondage, leather and rubber came in— but no dessert, only a dispiriting chapter on 'problems'. (The lack here of any sexual equivalent of a jam turnover or a tumescent soufflé is a disappointing lapse in an author whose elephantine humour can normally be relied upon.)

Dr Comfort was keen on the idea of the meal itself as an erotic experience. Like everybody else, he recalled the famous meal in the 1963 movie *Tom Jones*, where the two lovers consume their chicken and their fruit with a cannibalistic voracity that leaves us in no doubt as to what's going on or what's going to go on. (Though I might add that the erotic *use* of food, as opposed to the erotic eating of it—the smearing of yoghurt on the nether regions, the exchange of eggs from mouth to mouth as in the movie *Tampopo*—is something that I've never really approved of. It brings me over all prim and proper, and makes me want to remind people that there are poor children in Africa who would be glad of that food.)

Reliably, though, Dr Comfort got it wrong. Obsessed with sexual experience and the laborious cataloguing of its varieties, he was incapable of really seeing this or any other meal as an erotic experience. He thought this meal erotic because in the course of it, he said, the woman tries to excite the man with her display of oral aggression. In fact, it's clear that both diners are possessed of healthy appetites: their obvious enjoyment of the food is a sign by which each confirms to the other their mutual desire. But not even a two-way semiotic trade makes for an erotic meal, any more than a dirty phone call makes for erotic fibre optics.

The scene in *Tom Jones* is harmless and witty, but Alex Comfort's reaction to it, and to food in general, reveals him as something he never wanted to be: a Puritan, a fanatic for whom any human activity is worthwhile only if it serves some other, higher end, whether religious, political, or, as in Dr Comfort's case, sexual. The first Puritans, those of England in the sixteenth and seventeenth centuries, wanted Church services so purged of beauty that nobody would be tempted to enjoy them as aesthetic experiences in their own right. But no human activity is worthwhile unless seen in its own terms. A meal isn't truly worthwhile if it is seen only as a means to an end or as a sign of or metaphor for something else.

This is why I'm doubtful of the idea of the meal as an instrument of seduction. At least, I think this is why. I tell myself that hopes and fears about what's to come after the coffee will poison the food. I could, though, be kidding myself. Might it be that what I feel is not doubt but terror? Don't I dread being alone with nothing but empty plates and lipstick-rimmed glasses as reminders of what might have been and no prospects but the washing up and an early night with a good book?

My objection to food as a metaphor for sex is more soundly based. It's true, I admit, that everything in works of fiction is fair game for the metaphor-hunter; nothing can automatically be assumed to be inconsequential. In real life, an ugly face is just a bum deal in the lottery of existence. In fiction or film, it's likely to be interpreted as an outward and visible sign of inner moral corruption. Alternatively, we may find that the ugly character is of unblemished virtue, but this we're likely to interpret as the author's way of telling us that appearances can be misleading. In either case, we assume that a point is being made.

This is why food that is written about in novels or shown on film is seldom innocent. If the food's there for any purpose other than that of simply bringing the characters together, it's likely to be there as a sign of social status or a metaphor for sex.

Almost all of Laura Esquivel's excessively cute *Like Water for Chocolate* is a good example of this process. As a book and as a film (with a screenplay by the author), it's an exercise in user-friendly magical realism: there are no talking parrots, nobody discovers a ship in the depths of the jungle, and it has a great warm, gooey heart. It's the story of Tita, a Mexican woman born in the kitchen, the third of three daughters, denied marriage because family tradition dictates that, as youngest daughter, she must devote herself to the care of her widowed mother. Thwarted in love, Tita develops a passionate relationship with food. She's taught the arts of the kitchen by the family cook, a gnarled old peasant woman who says stupid gnarled-old-peasant-woman things, like 'only the pan knows how the boiling soup feels . . .' This is supposed to sound wise, like much that is said here about food. 'The secret is that, when you cook it, you cook it with much love,' says Tita in the film when somebody asks how she achieved one of her culinary triumphs. (That sort of thing is all very well, but it's no substitute for being told to take the whites of half a dozen eggs and beat them until peaks form.)

It's through food that Tita expresses her love for the man who loves her but has married her sister. He has given her roses, which she clutches so firmly to her bosom that her blood stains their pink petals red. Then she uses them to cook quails in rose petal sauce and, we're told, 'It was as if a strange alchemical process had dissolved her entire being in the rose petal sauce, in the tender flesh of the quails, in the wine, in every one of the meal's aromas.' The effect on her other sister is striking. Inflamed by the passion in the sauce, she dashes from the room in search of a shower, sets fire to the outhouse with the heat of her naked body, and has sex on a horse with a passing revolutionary.

Laura Esquivel provides her readers with this and

several other recipes, but it's doubtful whether they'd fool anybody, even if they were more reliable than they actually are: this is a novel about love and sex, not food and eating, and the meals—hot, passionate and lovingly cooked though they may be—are metaphorical meals. I'm still waiting for the novel or movie in which sex is a metaphor for eating. I already have a plot outline for anyone who might want to use it. The scene is the twenty-second century and the whole world has finally yielded to vegetarian pressure: meat-eating is illegal and punishable by the most severe penalties. The story concerns a young couple whose desire for animal flesh is so great that they can sublimate their gastronomic longings only with frequent, prolonged and sweaty bouts of bonking.

# W is for weather

'It was the usual Australian Christmas dinner, taking place in the middle of the day. Despite the temperature being 100°F in the shade, there had been the full panoply of ragingly hot food, topped off with a volcanic plum pudding smothered in scalding custard.' This is Clive James, talking about one of the Christmases of his early childhood, the one when Grandpa nearly choked on a sixpence in the pudding. 'Mentally,' says James of his decrepit grandsire, 'he had never left England.'

Neither had the food they were all eating. These were the 1940s: Australian food was still hot, heavy and stupefying, even though half a century had passed since a medical man of some standing had tried very hard to correct things. Shortly before Queen Victoria's Diamond Jubilee, this medical man had tried to persuade his compatriots away from their suety, English habits. He sought a greater cultivation of the garden, the vine, the deep-sea fishery, and he thought that if Australia was to have a national dish, it should be a salad. His name was Philip E. Muskett and his book, *The Art of Living in Australia*, was published in 1893.

'There is one important matter which unquestionably requires to have special attention drawn to it,' wrote Muskett, scarcely more than half a dozen pages into his treatise. 'I refer to the customary Australian mid-day meal. Strange to say, all through the hot season, as well as the rest of the year, this consists in most cases of a heavy repast always comprising meat.' In Sydney, he sadly observed, there were more than twice as many butchers as greengrocers. In New South Wales as a whole, the consumption of meat was greater, per head, than in any other country in the world. He patriotically looked forward to the day when this would no longer be so: a day when his country would 'reach the zenith of her possibilities' because her people had at last begun to live in accordance with their surroundings. It would be a land full of market gardens, vineyards and olive groves.

'One of the most extraordinary circumstances in connection with the Australian people is, that they have never yet realised their semi-tropical environment,' wrote Muskett. Like so many Australians of his time, he spoke of England as 'the old country', yet much of what this son of English parents wrote reveals an abiding frustration with Anglo-Saxon conservatism. Would the

English stolidly insist on eating the heaviest food in the midday sun no matter where Empire took them? Muskett thought they would, and he sadly envisaged English restaurants in Equatorial Africa offering 'roast beef, Yorkshire pudding, plum pudding, and the old familiar throng'.

This is unfair, and Muskett must have known that it was unfair. Whatever the English in Australia had been doing, whatever the English in equatorial Africa might do, the English in India had already shown themselves capable of at least trying to suit what they ate to where they were. It's true that by the time Muskett put pen to paper the English no longer had quite the taste for Indian food that they once had. But even in the early years of this century the gastronomic correspondent of the *Pall Mall Gazette* could tickle the nostalgia of an old India hand by showing him that the Cecil Hotel in London could lay on a very respectable *curry à l'indienne* complete with chutneys, relishes and poppadums. Indeed, 'currey' had been a feature of the English kitchen at least since Hannah Glasse's *Art of Cookery*, published in 1747, and Edward Abbot, author of the first Australian cookery book, is quite firm on the subject, preferring Malay curries to those of Bengal or Madras and insisting that 'a curry in a deluge of broth, with meats floating about like so many islands, is an abomination'.

But the English first arrived in India at the beginning of the seventeenth century, when their own cooking had barely emerged from a medieval reliance on heavy spicing, so they were able to acquire a taste for Indian food at a time before Indian food tasted really alien. Not until the nineteenth century did they feel secure enough to despise the food of the locals, and it was, of course, the cousins and colleagues of these imperial British who ran Australia in Muskett's day. When Muskett turned his attention to India, he saw not the British tucking into their meat curries but 'the Hindoos', who, he observed, subsisted largely on a diet of cereals. And this mattered to him because, wherever he looked in the world (provided he didn't look at Australia), he saw diets that were in accord with the climates in which they were eaten.

In mean annual temperature, he noted, Australia resembles the countries of the Mediterranean, and yet, while the diet of Southern Europe, rich in vegetables, 'is in rational harmony with its climate', that Australia consists largely of meat consumed in huge quantities: 'Thus the student of ethnography is presented with the somewhat curious anomaly of a people living in a summer temperature of 70 or 80°F in the shade eating more meat than do the bulk of the inhabitants of Great Britain and Ireland (with their ice and snow) during their winter months.'

Muskett—opinionated, quirky, dogmatic—is anxious to prove that he is not alone in his opinions. 'Many philosophical writers', he points out, have argued that the character of a people is moulded by the climate in which it lives, and he furnishes an impressive list of authorities: from his own century, the historian Buckle and the philosopher Comte, and, from the century before, David Hume, who was both historian and philosopher, together with the French political theorist Charles Louis de Secondat, Baron de La Brède et de Montesquieu.

This was heavy intellectual artillery to bring to bear on the butchers and plum puddings of Sydney. No one, of course, would want to suggest that Muskett had not made his happy way through Henry Thomas Buckle's *History of Civilisation in England* or all six volumes of Auguste Comte's *Cours de Philosophie Positive*. (The fact that he gets Comte's first name wrong is an indication, perhaps, that he didn't have his Comte to hand when he wrote his own book.) Nonetheless it's not immediately clear what use these writers can be to a Sydney medical man who's keen on salads.

Take Montesquieu for example. What comfort has he to offer an Englishman living in a hot climate? Montesquieu thought he had physiological reasons for arguing that people who lived in cold climates were braver, more vigorous, less cunning and suspicious than those who lived in the heat. In general, he said, they seemed to feel less ('You must flay a Muscovite alive to make him feel') but at the same time they were much less distracted by sex. Orientals, by contrast, were indolent in mind and body, and the lands in which they lived were given over to political despotism and fun in bed. The fun was, though, for men only. In hot climates women achieved an early physical maturity and were over the hill at twenty, so it was unknown for a woman to be sexually desirable and intellectually mature at the same time. The result was polygamy and the subjection of women.

Obviously, Philip Muskett didn't take his Montesquieu very seriously. If he had, he'd have returned to the land of his fathers, fearing for Australia a despotic, Arabian-Nights sort of future, full of wicked viziers, scheming eunuchs and sudden death. He'd have foreseen an Australia in which the men—workshy and oversexed, long since drained of their hardy, Northern virtues—would sit languidly on the beach waxing their surfboards, attended by very young and submissive women. A strange and foreign prospect.

In fact, not taking Montesquieu seriously (and not taking Buckle, Comte or Hume seriously either) is essential to what Muskett is doing. Montesquieu and the others were engaged in a serious proto-sociological pursuit: they were trying to discover universal truths of human nature. History and travellers' tales told them that people differed widely from time to time and from place to place; but surely, they thought, the fabric of humanity was the same everywhere and for all time? What, then, were the forces that gave to this fabric one shape in one place and a different shape in another? If humanity was constant and it was only places that differed across time and space, then it seemed reasonable to look at what it was that made one place different from another. Hence their interest in climate.

But the weather is not the only possible explanation for the character of a people. Perhaps it isn't the place that makes people what they are, but the chief product of the place, the food that feeds them. Why, for example (and these are not my examples), is the English worker superior to the Italian? Why are Indians so apathetic? Why did the German revolution of 1848 fail? Writing in 1850, the philosopher Ludwig Feuerbach thought that the answer to all these questions had a lot to do with diet: the English were better than the Italians because they ate roast beef; the Indians were so listless and impassive because they lived largely on vegetables; his fellow Germans couldn't manage a decent revolution because they had been made sluggish by too much potato and not enough of that seed of rebellion, the bean.

Reviewing a now-forgotten book on the science of food, Feuerbach rashly suggested that it and it alone could solve the most basic problems of metaphysics. Philosophers, he said, had long worried about the connection between body and soul, but the common people had always known from experience that there was no mystery about what kept the two together: 'Food becomes blood, blood becomes heart and brain, the stuff of thoughts and attitudes. Human sustenance is the basis of human education and attitudes. If you want to improve the people, then give it, in place of exhortations against sin, better food. *Man is what he eats.*'

The worst of it is that Feuerbach really does seem to have meant what he said: not that food plays a very important role in making you what you are, but that food *is* you. This is not helpful and it is a sad reflection on the standard of the cooking that must have been available to your average post-Hegelian materialist philosopher in mid-nineteenth-century Bavaria. Ignoring the pleasures of the table in all their variety, Feuerbach is interested only in food as fuel. To some extent, of course, he's right: you are what you eat in that you are proteins, carbohydrates, minerals, fats and, of course, water, but only obsessive dieters think of themselves as actually eating proteins, carbohydrates, minerals and fats. The rest of us eat tomatoes, lightly dressed with oil and pepper, spaghetti with a pesto sauce, *nasi goreng, bouillabaisse, pichelsteiner* (a German stew in which the enervating presence of potatoes can be relieved by some rabble-rousing beans). In short, we eat, and we think of ourselves as eating, not nutrients but particular foods or particular dishes.

This is why Brillat-Savarin was a wiser man than Feuerbach. A quarter of a century before Feuerbach told his readers that they were what they ate, Brillat-Savarin was exhorting *his* readers in the fourth of the twenty aphorisms with which he prefaces his *Physiology of Taste,* 'Tell me what you eat, and I shall tell you what you are.' The aphoristic manner—the brief utterance which seems neither to brook contradiction nor to invite reply—would perhaps have appealed to Feuerbach (he had been a university teacher, and the habits of the lecture hall, especially of the German lecture hall, die hard). So, no doubt, would the aphorism immediately before this one, which tells us that the fate of nations depends on how they nourish themselves. But Brillat-Savarin isn't writing about nourishment; he's writing about flavour. This, presumably, is why we are given no definition of food until quite some way into his book: food, considered as nourishment, is of less concern to him than food as a source of sensual and social pleasure. Brillat-Savarin knows that we are not merely constituted in a physiological sense but defined in a social sense by what we eat: it's the dressing of the dish, not its nutritional value, that tells me who you are. The idea is nicely summed up in the Thai expression, *gan gin gan yuu*: 'as you eat, so you are'.

If Brillat-Savarin got it right and Feuerbach got it wrong, this is perhaps because the Frenchman did not aspire to philosophical heights. An intelligent man who enjoyed good food, he simply wanted to write as intelligently as he could about what he enjoyed. Poor Philip Muskett, on the other hand, is a man less confident of his ambitions. There's no doubt that he got pleasure from what he ate—he wanted his compatriots to experiment with a wider range of vegetables, to enjoy salads as good as those eaten in France or at the very least to cook their meat more imaginatively—and there's no doubt that he thought, rightly, that better food would make for a better life in all sorts of ways. But a fearful uncertainty seizes him. He can't make sensible observations about the unsuitability of Yorkshire pudding to a Sydney summer and then let it alone; he just has to mix it with the likes of Hume and Montesquieu. The problem is not merely that they're out of his league but that they're in a different line of business. Their mode is descriptive: they want to explain the world; his mode is prescriptive: he wants to change it.

But he wants to change it only along certain lines, which is why the theorists he quotes serve him only for purposes of decoration. A clever disciple of Montesquieu might have told him that there was an intimate relationship between climate, food and culture. Was the hot, scented polity of the Ottoman Turks tyrannical? Well, so was their food: it was a labour-intensive cuisine, requiring hours of chopping and pounding by minions (or wives) in the kitchen. To the best of my knowledge, Montesquieu didn't actually say this—and it's not necessarily true, anyway—but it would have been consistent with those things that he did say and which Muskett ignores.

Philip Edward Muskett wasn't a prophet and he wasn't a man born ahead of his time, but he was visionary. He saw variety where others saw sameness and gardens where they saw abattoirs. And, in suiting the cuisine to the climate but ignoring the culture, he was a portent of eating in twentieth-century Australia.

# X is for Xanadu

When I was a boy in England, the most expensive meat we ever had was chicken.

The magical evocation of childhood, whether literary or cinematic, is a loathsome genre. There are no blue remembered hills in what I care to recall of my infancy, no picturesque poverty, no eccentric uncles: I have never felt the rude comradeship of the tenement or the village, the solidarity which draws the poor together in fraternal embrace. It just wasn't like that: conscious neither of rough warmth nor of serious deprivation, totally ignorant of what the rest of the world ate, all I knew was that chicken was expensive and we didn't have it very often. I don't remember much about beef, but I do remember that we had lamb and pork more often than we had chicken.

A lot of current has flown through the hen house

since then (stunning the birds so that their throats can be peacefully slit and their bodies eviscerated) and now chicken is one of the cheaper kinds of meat. For a long time, though, even when I knew that chickens and bits of chicken could be plentifully obtained for small outlay, it still tasted expensive to me. No matter how much of it I ate, or how little I had spent on it, sitting down to a plate of chicken (and especially roast chicken) was like sitting down to a special occasion.

What if it had been the other way round? What if chickens had been abundant and cheap when I was young and now were few and expensive—would an air of poverty and of making-do still hang about these rare birds? I doubt it; in the world of food, upward mobility seems to be faster than downward mobility. The world of food is welcoming and forgiving; it will readily forget your humble origins, providing you're rare and expensive.

The oyster is probably the most famous example of a comestible *arriviste*: 'poverty and oysters always seem to go together ...' says Sam Weller in *Pickwick Papers*. That was in 1837, just a few years before over-consumption nearly drove the English oyster to extinction and placed it beyond the reach of all but the rich. (As an immigrant to Australia, I find that my personal history of oysters echoes that of the chook: they still taste special to me, even though I'm now nearly in a position to test Grimod de la Reynière's claim that they cease to whet the appetite after the first seven dozen.) But the case of caviar is even more striking than that of oysters. It demonstrates that you don't have to be rare and expensive to be highly thought of: you just have to be expensive.

I once went to a caviar tasting, and I have to say I felt pretty damn bad about it. I'm not sure why the idea of going to one of Sydney's smarter restaurants and consuming large quantities of caviar and champagne at someone else's expense should have made me feel guilty—Heaven knows, it's not as though I'm unaccustomed to costly free-loading—but it undoubtedly did. Perhaps it had something to do with caviar's status as such an obvious, almost banal, symbol of the high life. The very thought of it brings to mind those gaudy Russian caricatures from the early days of Bolshevism: pictures of capitalists who really look like capitalists, corpulent men wearing big black silk hats, smoking fat cigars, riding around in Rolls Royces and grinding the faces of the poor. They're the sort of people who eat caviar.

The Russians ought to know: it is they who are responsible for the high price of Beluga caviar and for the fact that the Beluga is now close to being an endangered species. 'The days of Beluga are over,' according to the man who ran the tasting, Babak Hadi, Australian General Manager of Black Pearl Caviar. He meant the caviar. The fish itself, one of the three species of sturgeon whose roe (or eggs) are drained and pressed to make this expensive commodity, may still be in with a chance: the annual catch of Beluga from the Caspian is now fewer than a hundred fish.

It didn't used to be like this. At the beginning of the century, Sevruga was the most popular variety, preferred for its stronger flavour. So the enterprising Russians tripled the price of Beluga overnight. Its popularity increased sharply, there was massive fishing and, then, overfishing. This sort of thing happens quite often at the penthouse level of the food and drink business, where (in a perverse upending of the canons of economic orthodoxy) demand is determined by high prices, rather than vice versa. The Champenoise have always known this and have been careful to locate their product at the top end of the market.

If the American food writer Waverley Root is to be believed, the fate of caviar has been very similar to that of the oyster. He relates how caviar was used in American saloons the way modern bars use peanuts: it was there on the counter, free for any drinker who wanted to nibble it (and, as result, become more thirsty). By the 1890s, though, caviar was already established as a luxury item, with the consequence, says Root, that 'since Russian caviar had long held the most enviable reputation, canny French caviar makers shipped kegs of their product to Russia, whence it returned bedecked with Russian labels, permitting French gourmets to eat French caviar at the price of the imported article'.

Such trickery is not unknown even today. According to Babak, Beluga is now so rare that much of what is sold as Beluga is in fact another variety, Osietra. 'It's fairly well known with anyone who deals with caviar,' he told us at the tasting. 'But there's not really anything we can do about it, because people are fixated on Beluga.'

To be fixated on rarity is, I suppose, natural enough; to be fixated on expense is just plain vulgar. I love caviar—at the tasting I eagerly shovelled down the fresh Iranian Sevruga as though it were taramasalata—but there is something very embarrassing about the company it keeps: 'From those meals I recall eating something that looked like an upmarket Big Mac, consisting of layers of thick pancake, smoked salmon, sour cream, and caviar, and something called "crisp shrimp with mustard fruits", which came surrounded with a cold fatty batter that any suburban Chinese restaurant would be ashamed to put around its prawn cutlets.' This is David Dale—in the late 1980s, the *Sydney Morning Herald*'s man in New York— eating at a fashionable Manhattan restaurant. The Big Mac *manqué* is recognisable as a hypertrophied version of an old classic from the days of Escoffier's Russophilia, *caviar aux blinis.* This is one of the dishes that Charles Ryder and Rex Mottram eat when they dine together at a Parisian restaurant in *Brideshead Revisited.* Charles adds it to the menu at the last minute, fearing that otherwise the whole thing will be too simple for Rex. So it seems that a dish that in times past could be guaranteed to tickle the palate of a rich vulgarian, just wasn't rich or vulgar enough for the Manhattan of Donald Trump. They simply *had* to tack on a few extra storeys.

It was from David Dale that I stole the idea of writing about Xanadu:

> In Xanadu did Kubla Khan
> A stately pleasure dome decree

The story of Coleridge's *Kubla Khan* is well known. He published this poem, he claimed, 'as a psychological curiosity', having composed it while in a sleep induced by some medical drug he had taken. He describes the 'gardens bright with sinuous rills' in language self-consciously (or, if we believe the author, unconsciously) lush and rich, but unfortunately we do not get to learn about the rich delicacies the great Khan ate in his pleasure dome; the person from Porlock interrupted the poet just when he had turned to food:

> For he on honey-dew hath fed,
> And drunk the milk of Paradise.

This is not a reference to melons; like nectar, honey-dew seems to be more an idea of sweetness than a real substance. Its very vagueness of reference suits a poem in which wealth and power are evoked in such a dreamlike way.

In fact, the Xanadu that David Dale had in mind was not Samuel Taylor Coleridge's but Charles Foster Kane's: the dreamlike castle that he built ('Cost: No man can say') on the coast of Florida and that he filled with the loot of the world but did not live to complete. The closing shots of *Citizen Kane*, best remembered for showing us the destruction of Rosebud, are a panorama of this useless accumulation: statues, furniture, a painting attributed to Donatello and countless crates as yet unpacked. What did Charles Foster Kane eat? The movie offers little evidence, but it's reasonable to assume that, as a rich man, he feasted (at least when guests were present) on rich man's food. This is the culinary equivalent of the loot with which he filled his castle, rich things avidly gathered from here and there and thrown together: caviar, truffles, ortolans.

These things don't change very much. In the first century, Petronius had his Charles Foster Kane, the self-made plutocrat Trimalchio, treat his guests to many a rich thing stuffed with other rich things; and he made him boast about having a cook who could make lard look like pigeon and a sow's belly look like fish. But in the freer air of the American empire, one democratic detail has crept in. David Dale has been to Xanadu—San Simeon, home of the newspaper magnate William Randolph Hearst, generally agreed to have been Kane's original— and he reports that the dinner table is, as you'd expect, huge and laden with silver. But at intervals along its great length, Hearst, attentive to his guests' every desire, had placed sauce. Commercial brown sauce, still in the bottle, still with the labels on.

# y is for yam

'Bush all round—bush with no horizons, for the country is flat. No ranges in the distance. The bush consists of stunted, rotten native apple-trees. No undergrowth. Nothing to relieve the eye save the darker green of a few she-oaks which are sighing above the narrow, almost waterless creek.'

Not many verbs. A disciplined monotone, harsh and spare to reflect the landscape it describes: a harsh, spare terrain, instilling a grim discipline in those who try to make a living out of it. The famous opening of Henry Lawson's story, 'The Drover's Wife'.

It's almost superfluous to point out that this is the language of someone for whom the Australian bush is a dwelling place but not a home. Verbs imply possibility, action, growth, and there is little of those things here.

But how would the scene look to the three Aboriginal

characters who are allowed walk-on roles in the narrative? What would King Jimmy, Black Mary ('the "whitest" gin in all the land') and a certain unreliable 'stray black-fellow' think? It's at least possible that they, surveying this bright implacable bushland, would see something quite different: a landscape to be depicted not in a harsh monotone but with a rich and sensuously wandering line; a landscape rich in possibilities, in things to eat that the white fellows wouldn't touch and in secret, hidden, life-sustaining yams.

The food of hunter-gatherer cultures is, by its very nature, hidden from the casual observer. The food of pastoralists is real and has four legs, the food of agriculturalists is real estate, but the food of hunter-gatherers is not something that covers the landscape. Instead, their food *is* the landscape. Their food yields itself most abundantly only to those who know what to look for.

There is no better emblem for all this invisible food than the yam, many varieties of which are eaten by Aboriginal people in Australia. 'The digging of a yam takes skill and determination,' writes Jennifer Isaacs in her book on bush food, 'particularly if the leaves are no longer visible and the dead parts above ground are simply dried, twining tendrils.'

What, if anything, I wonder, did the Irish settlers of Australia make of the Aboriginal relationship with the yam? Did it remind them of the potato, first the tuberous saviour of their nation and then, when the blight came, its curse? The potato too can be a hidden food. Traditionally, the Irish cultivated the spud by what was known as 'the lazy-bed system': you spread manure over a strip of land and set your potatoes on the manure; then you dig up the turf on either side of the strip and lay it face down on the manure; as the young potato plants begin to appear, you cover them loosely with further turves. Now, whatever happens to you or your land, your potato tubers are pretty safe. You may be overrun by another clan or by the English soldiers of Cromwell or William of Orange, and they may destroy any young potato plants that dare to show their heads above ground, but your future crop is still assured.

Once the food gets onto the plate, or into the hand, it ceases to be hidden. Or, at least, it ought to, but there is a sense in which those of us who gaze in ignorance and fear at the bush are still missing the point when we look at what the rest of the world eats. Just as we don't notice the tuberous, starchy roots that are hidden underground, so we don't notice the fact that what most cultures value about their food is its starchy foundation.

Take rice, for example. 'A proper meal is inconceivable without it,' says David Thompson in his *Classic Thai Cuisine*. 'All other dishes, curries, salads, whatever else is on the table, are called *gap kao*, with rice.' Rice is the sustenance, the meal, and everything else is a condiment to it, adding moisture, texture, interest.

It's the same story in China. A proper Chinese meal

is a balance between *fan* (rice, corn or millet) and *ts'ai* (meat and vegetables) but the balance is always in favour of *fan*. The meat and veg are there for the purpose of *hsia fan*, to assist the intake of *fan*, and good Chinese children learn to ask for lots of *fan* and very little *ts'ai*. The word *fan* is more or less synonymous with food: to have a job is to have 'the grains to chew', to lose one is to have 'broken the rice bowl'.

Even in our Chinese restaurants—whose proprietors politely refrain from forcing on us their native philosophy of food—the higher status of *fan* is made clear by the fact that everybody gets a rice bowl; the meat and veg, on the other hand, are shared, just as you might share a salt cellar or a bottle of sauce.

All over the world, with very few exceptions (and one large exception, which I'll come to shortly) the centre of the meal is *fan*, not just rice but starch in any one of a wide variety of forms: bread, potatoes, yams, noodles, pasta or various kinds of glutinous goo, like the famous *poi* that Hawaiians make from the starchy root taro, and, of course, porridge. 'Porridge is food, it makes you strong,' they used to say in what is now Ghana. The porridge was always accompanied by a soup flavoured with meat or red pepper, but everybody agreed that, though you might overdose on soup, you could never have too much porridge.

A Southern Bantu people called the Bemba ate porridge too, and their attitude to it was exactly that of the

Chinese: for *fan* read *ubwali*, porridge made of millet, and for *ts'ai* read *umunani*, the relish of vegetables, meat or fish eaten with it as an aid to digestion.

The big exception to the almost-universal rule is, of course, the English-speaking world (and perhaps Argentina too). People in England and the U.S. used to eat lots of starch—bread and potatoes, with meat when they could afford it—but over the last hundred years or so, they, and their cultural cousins in Australia and New Zealand, have increasingly edged it to the side of the plate. You can tell what we think of carbohydrate by the marginal position it's given on the menu in American restaurants: pride of place goes to great hunks of animal protein, while rice, potatoes and the like are shuffled away into a little bargain basement labelled 'starch'.

It could be that we're less virtuous than the rest of the world; or it could be that we're just doing what the rest of the world would do if it had the money. After all, would the Chinese praise children who eat more *fan* than *ts'ai* if they didn't expect their kids to prefer the meat and veg to the stodge? On the other hand, it may be that learning to be Chinese—or Thai or Bemba—means learning to appreciate the solid foundation of starch that underlies your society.

# Z is for zakuski

I do not have a sweet tooth. I am quite capable of enjoying sweet things—especially ice cream and white chocolate—but the sweetness of dessert usually comes as an anti-climax to me. Having spent the previous hour or so enjoying the rich dark browns and burgundies of meat, subfusc vegetable greens and piscine silvers, stark and modernistic, I can never help feeling that the sweet course has suddenly ushered me into the nursery: bright primary colours to attract the wandering attention of the very, very young.

We associate sweetness with the end of the meal because it is an appetite inhibitor. An English practise of the last century provides a sad demonstration of this. In the 1880s, it seems, the farm labourers of rural England used to eat a sweet pudding made of fruit, currants or jam *before* their bacon and vegetables. There usually wasn't much bacon to go round and they knew that the sweet pudding would take the edge off their appetite.

But despite the physiological reasons for reserving most of the sweet things until the end of the meal, there are cultures where sweetness turns up much earlier on and in considerable quantities. I have had a Japanese meal in which the first course consisted of various vegetables together with whitebait, all coated in a thick, sticky, sweet glaze. The sweetened fish were particularly striking. This was not the sort of sweetness that we usually feel able to tolerate with meat or fish, that subtle hint of sugar in those sauces we describe as sweet and sour. Still less was it like the gentle, sweet perfume of vanilla with which the French chef Alain Sendrens notoriously partnered lobster in *nouvelle cuisine* days (I haven't tasted this dish but I have had prawns cooked with a vanilla sauce that beautifully picked up the sweetness of the crustacea). No, this was a rich, uncompromising, sugary sweetness. It was, to the Occidental tongue, a dessert sweetness. It was with me for as long as the fish and vegetables were with me and vanished with the first mouthful of the miso soup that came next.

A sweetness so distinct and yet so fragile is not out of place at the beginning of a meal. Besides, a Japanese meal is not, like a European meal, a steady progress from light, savoury things to heavy, savoury things and thence to light, sweet things. Just as the Japanese plate lacks a focal point—which for us usually means a large central lump of animal protein—so the Japanese banquet seems to have no hierarchy of dishes. It's just one thing after another. The order of things is no doubt carefully calculated, but—as with Japanese music, which to us seems just to go on for a bit and then stop—there is no sense of overture, climax, and anti-climax.

In Western meals, the sensation of sweetness, once it has arrived, is not easily banished. Instead, it banishes all other flavors, which is why I don't like it much: I want to be left with the taste of meat and vegetables in my mouth or I want it supplanted only by the bitterness of coffee. I would rather end a meal with an hors d'oeuvre than with a sweet pudding and I've tried to do so a couple of times, but without much success. At a Chinese restaurant, I ordered soup to finish with—which seemed rather a Chinese thing to do—but they obviously thought this odd of me. Then, at another restaurant meal with friends, I asked for a Caesar salad while they were ordering their trifles and mudcakes. I enjoyed it, but I did look as though I was trying to make some sort of statement, which I wasn't.

Perhaps I should stick to Japanese meals or alternatively to those meals in which the diner is invited to graze over a long table laden with many small things. This, in fact, is M.F.K. Fisher's solution to another gastronomic problem, the mirror image of mine: not an indifference to dessert, but an excessive love of hors d'oeuvres. For her, a rich array of hors d'oeuvres—'the tempting spicy smells, the clashing flavors'—is an invitation to such over-indulgence at the beginning of the meal that little appetite will remain for what follows. 'Even so,' she continues, 'it is fun now and then to roam uninhibited and unhurried through a smörgasbord, a buffets russe, hors d'oeuvres variés, however it may be called.'

I like that umlaut in 'smörgasbord'. Though the correct spelling is really 'smörgåsbord', the umlaut does at least suggest that, for her, the word had an integrity, a specificity of reference that it has since lost. We can assume that she would, quite rightly, have expected a smörgåsbord (literally a 'bread-and-butter table') to be an array of many things, including hard bread, eggs, cheese, potatoes, caviar, smoked meats and fish, raw and pickled. She would have known that a smörgåsbord isn't just any old buffet; she would have known that there is no such thing as a Chinese smörgåsbord, and that if there were, it wouldn't be the thing that goes by that name in Australian cities: an unprepossessing rank of *bains maries* in which various parodies of one of the world's greatest cuisines sit stewing all the live-long day.

The classical smörgåsbord is similar to the Russian zakuski, and 'zakuski' is the word that catches M.F.K. Fisher's attention when she turns to hors d'oeuvres; though she 'has never had them in the classical way', she says:

The nearest I came to that was when I used to go to a small cellar-restaurant behind the Russian Church in Paris, after

Sunday morning services. I always stopped in the bar and drank one or two vodkas and ate pressed caviar, the black at about eight francs if it had been a flush week, the red at five francs if it had been a thin one.

The Russian Church in Paris, the poor but happy *vie de bohéme*, caviar at five francs a throw, and who is that drinking vodka at the bar? Why, none other than the great Russian bass Feodor Chaliapin! It's a wonder Ernest Hemingway doesn't turn up. Why can't I have memories as classy as this?

The only time *I* ever had zakuski (not, of course, in the classical way) was on a Saturday night in the Bondi Masonic Hall. Some sort of Russian club met there every week to eat and dance. I remember plump matrons and old men in stiff, cheap suits moving slowly but skilfully to music that, strangely, seemed to be Greek. What I don't remember very well is the food. There was indeed a parade of hors d'oeuvres—I remember that—but tragically few of the neurons which saw active service that night seem to have survived the onslaught of the vodka. Almost all I can recall now is that, very much later that evening (or perhaps the following morning) I climbed up onto a flat roof high above Bondi and saw the limitless, phosphorescent ocean, which seemed so close that it was like an extension of the tarmac under my feet. I felt that I could have walked out through the mist and over the water. My only other memory is of an almost pathetically grateful taxi driver, to whom I must have given a very large tip indeed.

Vodka also features in M.F.K. Fisher's account of zakuski, though it seems to have done less damage to her Sunday morning than it did to my Saturday night. After catching sight so unexpectedly of the greatest bass singer of the century, she needed a stiff drink. 'It was a strange moment in my life,' she writes, 'as strong and good as the taste of caviar on my tongue and the bite of vodka in my throat.' (So Hemingway *was* there, after all.) It's not for the likes of me to make light of the intensity of Ms Fisher's experiences or of the literary skill with which she recorded them, but what about the lingering suspicion that the experiences, perfectly formed, conveniently appropriate, were an artefact of the literary skill? I don't mean that she made them up, but that she had them in order to write about them or that the literary memory—an elaborate structure of spun sugar—was larger, brighter, in some sense more real, than whatever remained on the inward eye.

Well, if she wrote more than she had experienced, so much the better for her readers; and the suspicion that she did what she did so that she could write what she wrote is unworthy. The fact is that any memoir will, if it's worth reading at all, have about it an air both of inevitability and of surprise. It should be impossible for the reader to think of what has been written about except in the words the author uses. The description and the experience described will become inseparable and so, naturally, the impression will be created that the experience was had only in order to justify the description of it. And this highly wrought fusion of word and object is, it goes without saying, as rare in the literature of food as good Mexican restaurants are outside Mexico. The literature of food is full of flat descriptions of experiences which were had solely in order that they could be written about. They're the payback for the business-class air tickets, the hotel room with the complimentary bottle of champagne, the long lunches and the dinners, the endless, endless dinners.

M.F.K. Fisher was never this sort of food writer. It's true that she wrote regularly for a magazine, but it was the austere *New Yorker*, never a great gatherer-up of PR freebies. Her very first book, *Serve it Forth* (published in 1937), begins with a subject rarely touched on by writers about food: hunger. Most food writers seem to think that somehow the food about which they write has got nothing to do with the stuff that actually sustains life. Ms Fisher never suffered from this strange dissociation of sensibility. 'When a man is small, he loves and hates food with a ferocity which soon dims,' she began in 1937. 'At six years old his very bowels will heave when such a dish as creamed carrots or cold tapioca appears before him.'

Even as early as this (Fisher was twenty-nine when the book appeared) the tone of voice is firm and unmistakable. Typical Fisher characteristics are already making themselves known: the long and accurate memory, reaching back to the earliest experiences of food and the need for it; the willingness to write about such little-regarded things as cold tapioca; and the preference for a masculine noun over an impersonal pronoun. When not writing in the first person, Fisher always prefers the masculine gender, even where neither the meaning nor the rhythm of the sentence seems to demand it: an aspect, perhaps, of that old-world formality which caused Mary Frances Kennedy Fisher to hide her sex behind a set of initials, and which, when she is not being confessional, gives an agreeably distant, mandarin air to her writing.

By 1949, though, her tone was mostly relaxed and anecdotal. She could even happily write of herself as a woman; and not just a woman but 'blessed among women' in that she had found someone with whom she so much wanted to spend her time that, if he was not there, dining alone would be preferable to dining with others. This was in *An Alphabet for Gourmets*, which begins with 'A is for dining Alone' and ends wittily with a selection of entrées, 'Z is for Zakuski'. I've stolen the idea. from her partly because it helps me over a difficult letter—I have nothing to say about *zabaglione* or *zuppa inglese*—but most of all in tribute to the wit and grace of one of the greatest food writers in our language.

# references

This book is not intended to be a work of scholarship, so it would be pretentious of me to furnish it with a thick and luxuriant carpet of footnotes. However, I do want to redeem my debts. In what follows, I try to give a general idea of where my ideas and facts have come from. The more easily traced references (to works both mentioned in the text and listed in the bibliography) have been omitted.

## a is for apple

The rules for the monastic breakfast are laid down in the Rule of St Benedict, viii and xi; see Bettenson, pp. 117 & 122. For the British breakfast and its role in history, I have relied mostly on Palmer. The account of Victorian breakfasts is based on Freeman, pp. 178–179, and Carlier, p. 24. The account of a bush breakfast is from Walker and Roberts, p. 26. McGee (1986), pp. 246–249, is useful and fascinating on the subject of breakfast cereals.

## b is for boundary

'The principal reason . . .': quoted in Harris, p. 68. My remarks about nature, culture and cooking owe much to Murcott, who in turn cites the anthropologist Edmund Leach, who in his turn is explicating Lévi-Strauss. The story of how the Roman Catholic Church managed to define the doctrine of transubstantiation in such a way as to preclude any suggestion of cannibalism is told in Bettenson, pp. 147–148. The anonymous fifteenth-century poem is from Davies (ed.), pp. 202–204. My remarks about Greek sacrifices derive from Detienne and Vernant, chs i–ii, and Goldhill, pp. 66–73. For the Canadian farmer, see Kalčik, p. 49. 'According to Beth Shammai . . .': The Babylonian Talmud, Tract Betzah (Yom Tob), ch. ii.

## c is for camel

For the camel as food, I have relied largely on Root, pp. 45–46. 'nameless meat and unusual horns': Emile Goncourt in Goncourt, p. 179. 'It's a kind of myth that a lot of people . . .': Dr Jennie Brand Miller addressing a press conference at the Fifteenth International Congress of Nutrition, Adelaide, September 1993. 'a part of all the rhythms . . .': Barthes (1973), p. 63. 'The Germans chew with the mouth closed . . .': C. Calviac, *Civilité* (1560), quoted in Elias, p. 91. My short list of Southern Italian regional delights is drawn from a paper on 'The Special Features of Southern Italian Cuisine and Wines', delivered by Valentina Harris to a seminar organised by the International Olive Oil Council in Sydney, 14 April, 1994. For Artusi's nationalism, see Roden (1989), p. 75.

## e is for exotic

'mixing little with the modern world . . .': quoted in Glenn R. Conrad, 'The Acadians: Myth and Realities', in Conrad (ed.), p. 1. The reference to the early eating of gumbo is from James H. Dormon, 'The Cajuns: Ethnogenesis and the Shaping of Group Consciousness', in Conrad (ed.) p. 240. For gumbo, see Ancelet, Edwards and Pitre, pp. 136–142. The reference to the Choctaw Indians is from *The Pica-yune's Creole Cook Book*, p. 35. My source for the information that things seemed to have hotted up is a conversation with Mathé Allain of the University of South West Louisiana. 'I remember when I was a kid . . .': Paul Prudhomme, interviewed by Martin Gillam on *The Food Program*, ABC Radio National, 17 September, 1989. For 'Cajun beer' see Barry Jean Ancelet's forward to Gutierrez, p. vii. I was told about the melding of the two cuisines by Carl Brasseaux of the University of South West Louisiana. The reference to the banquet is from Collins and Collins, p. 16. For gumbo at Antoine's, see the menus reproduced in Guste, pp. 17–19, 21–23. For Escoffier's way with peasant food see David, pp. 249–50. 'That's when gumbo is really gumbo,': quoted in Burton and Lombard, p. 10. 'I'm even sorrier that Cajuns . . .': Ancelet, foreword to Gutierrez, p. viii. 'You didn't hear so much . . .': quoted in Gutierrez, p. 16.

### f is for fire

'This their place of dwelling . . .': William Dampier, quoted in Pyne, p. 84. 'not only does cooking mark . . .': Lévi-Strauss, p. 164. On fugu chefs, see Satterwhite, pp. 64–65, and Richie, pp. 44–48. For McGee on the Maillard reaction, see McGee (1992), pp. 297–313. 'There has never . . .', quoted in MacDonogh, p. 180 (Grimod's mention of sealing in the juices is an early example of a fallacy that McGee (pp. 13–21) attributes to a later writer, Justus von Liebig). There are useful accounts of eighteenth- and nineteenth-century attempts to control heat in Brears, *et al.*, and Rossotti.

### g is for gross

'it is always possible that the currency . . .': Levy, p. 101. I am also grateful to Levy's essay for drawing my attention to the report in the *Asian Wall Street Journal* and to Derek Cooper's article in *The Listener*, 1 March, 1983. 'we haven't eaten anything raw . . .': Ken Hom, inter-viewed by Cherry Ripe on *The Food Program*, ABC Radio National, 18 August, 1988.

# h is for Hawaii

'King Sugar and his son Pineapple': Fred W. Beckley, testifying to a U.S. Congressional sub-committee in 1935 and quoted in Daws, p. 334. For an account of the early cultivation and export of Hawaiian sugar, see Tate, pp. 19–26. 'It will be better for the colored man ...': *Planters' Monthly*, 1886, quoted in Daws p. 213. The mutual fears of cannibalism among the British and the Hawaiians are discussed in Obeyesekere, pp. 138–139. 'The ladies are very lavish of their favours ...': William Ellis, Surgeon's Mate on the *Resolution*, quoted in Sahlins (1981), p. 39, who also gives (pp. 46–55) an account of the breaking of the food *kapus*. 'We intend that the husband's food ...': quoted in Sahlins (1981), p. 63. 'but was evidently much perturbed.': from an account given by Kaahumana to the Rev. A. Bishop in 1826 and quoted in Kuykendall, p. 68 (Obeyesekere suggests, p. 229, n. 8, that this account 'is probably mythicised'). 'an economy of determinate ends ...': Sahlins (1992), p. 29. 'well formed ... capable of bearing great fatigue': William Ellis, 1832, and James King, 1779, quoted in Shintani and Hughes, eds., pp. 8–9. There is a discussion of chiefly obesity in Sahlins (1992), p. 78–81. 'My mother was typical Hawaiian ...': Eleanor Harvey in Kodama-Nishomoto, Nishimoto and Oshiro, eds., p. 39.

# i is for ink

'What was the point ...': Eisenstein, p. 65 (who also discusses, pp. 243–252, the welter of instructional manuals published from the sixteenth century onwards). As well as Willan, Jeanneret (pp. 85–87) and Revel (pp. 117–119) also have useful accounts of Platina's work. For the cooking of roux, see Gutierrez, pp. 52–53. 'O ye immortal Gods ...': quoted in Willan, p. 23 (there is a discussion of *biancomangiare*, and a modern version of Martino's recipe, in Riley, p. 26).

# j is for Japan

The sad-faced man is a caricature (not, I hope, an unkind one) of the late Roland Barthes, and the whole of this section is a dialogue on what he has to say about Japanese food in Barthes (1982). The observation about the Argonauts is from Barthes (1977), p. 46. There are no direct

# a is for apple

quotations from Barthes here; everything is my paraphrase, and my paraphrase is by no means always reliable. The details about Japanese cuisine are drawn from Richie and Satterwhite.

## k is for kitchen

For Chinese cookshops, see Michael Freeman, 'Sung', in Chang (ed.), pp. 162–163. 'It is as difficult to put together ...': quoted in Mac-Donogh, p. 192.

## l is for liquamen

For Mongol food and the Chinese attitude to it, see Frederick W. Mate, 'Yüan and Ming', in Chang (ed.), pp. 203–210. 'Cajuns make better lovers ...': quoted by Barry Jean Ancelet in Gutierrez, p. ix; see p. 128 for the Cajuns' horror at Vietnamese food habits. For Grimod's sauce and his biographer's shock at *liquamen*, see MacDonogh, p. 132. 'I have been told that Soy is made ...': William Dampier (1699) quoted in *The Oxford English Dictionary*, entry for 'Soy'. The correctness of William Dampier's gentleman friend is usefully made clear in a diagram in Mollison, p. 69, who devotes a whole chapter to fermented fish, and tackles *garum* and British anchovy paste on pp. 137–138. McGee (1986), pp. 39–40, is useful on food and decay. For *murri*, see Charles Perry, 'Medieval Near Eastern Rotted Condiments', in Jaine (ed.), pp. 169–177. 'the kind that stinks in a Byzantine jar': Horace, *Epodes*, 2.2.66, quoted in Gowers, p. 156. Apicius' recipe for stuffed dormice is given by Giacosa, p. 75, who also describes the farming of the animals. The commentator mentioned here is Gowers, who discusses, pp. 70–75, stuffed dormice and the prejudice against stuffed things in general. 'thereby apparently exalting ...': quoted in Jeanneret, p. 28. Apicius' recipe for saving *liquamen* is reproduced in Giacosa, p. 181.

## m is for music

For Rossini's culinary tastes, see Weinstock, pp. 215, 251, 270–272, 328, and for *tournedos Rossini* see Revel, p. 240. 'a most inconvenient bird ...': quoted in Keates, p. 265. See Fisher, p. 643, for her mental enjoyment of recipes. For food in French tales of the early middle ages, see Page (1987), pp. 154–155; for later literature, see Page (1982) and, for the Feast of the Pheasant, Wheaton, pp. 1–9. 'took delight not so much in food and wine . . .': Adam of Bremen, quoted in Dronke, p. 27. For Plato's views on cookery and on food, see, respectively, his *Gorgias* and his *Republic*. 'The courses of the great banquet . . .': Pierfrancesco Giambullari, in Minor and Mitchell, p. 136. For feasts at the Ming court, see Frederick W. Mote in Chang (ed.), pp. 219–20. For Ficino, see Jeanneret, pp. 20–21. For the Sforza wedding, see Jenny Neville, 'The Musical Banquet in *Quattrocento* Festivities', in Corones, Pont and Santich (eds), p. 130, and for 'The Pleasures of the Enchanted Isle', see Wheaton, pp. 129–133, and Pont, 'In Search of the *Opera Gastronomica*', in Corones, Pont and Santich (eds), pp. 118–122. The book-learned English cook is Alastair Little and his embarrassment is described by Bateman.

**n is for nature**
'It is an honest cooking, too . . .': David (1950), p. 16. The discussion of the 'Optimal Traditional Mediterranean Diet' is drawn from the report of a conference held at Harvard in 1992 under the auspices of the Oldways Foundation. 'Warming by an open fire . . .': quoted in Cowan, p. 56. My observations about vegetarianism and health food shops were suggested by Murcott, pp. 112–114.

**o is for offal**
'there is much more steak . . .': Sahlins (1976), p. 176. On Bovril and its catch phrases, see Rees, p. 129.

**p is for politics**
'The man with whom I do not dine . . .': quoted in Gowers, p. 26 (see also pp. 213–214 for the host as king). On dinner etiquette in Louis XIV's time, see Wheaton, pp. 141–142. There is a fascinating account of Dutch banquets and the sumptuary laws in Schama, pp. 178–186. 'running to pages in their detail . . .': Gowers, p. 21. For the sumptuary

# a is for apple

regulations of revolutionary China, see Chang (ed.), p. 15, and, for banquets at the Ming court, Frederick W. Mote, in Chang (ed.), pp. 218–220. For Curnonsky, see Mennell, p. 328. For fascist food, see Bertram M. Gordon, 'Fascism, the Neo-Right and Gastronomy: A Case in the Theory of the Social Engineering of Taste', in Jaine (ed.), pp. 82–97. For the hot dog, see Bruce Kraig, 'The American Hot Dog: Standardised Taste and Regional Variations', in Jaine (ed.), pp. 108–113.

# q is for qualia

This chapter owes a lot to my own dialogue on the subject of taste with Michael O'Mahony, Professor of Food Science and Technology at the University of California, and to a paper he gave in 1994 at the Sensory Research Centre of the CSIRO Division of Food Research. There is an account of taste, the fifth flavour and the work of the ingenious physicians in McGee (1986), pp. 560–570.

# r is for revolution

On *cuisine minceur*, see Levy, pp. 36, 57–63, 144. '*Vive la Nouvelle Cuisine Française*': quoted in Barr and Levy, p. 62. The French magazine is *Paris Poche*, cited in Bailey, p. 193, and Revel, p. 9. On the fading from fashion of the term *nouvelle cuisine*, see Michael Symons, 'A Gastronomy of Nouvelle Cuisine', in Santich and Symons (eds), p. 67. 'every meat presented . . .': Lady Morgan (1831), quoted in Mennell, p. 147 (original capitalised throughout).

# s is for saunders

On the social climbing fellow of Merton, see Salter. Flora Thompson's account of calf's foot jelly is quoted in Driver, p. 166. On 'made-up' dishes, see Freeman, p. 125. 'these arrogant and greedy islanders . . .': quoted in MacDonogh, p. 179. 'The art of cooking . . .': Pehr Kalm, quoted in Porter, p. 234. On meals dedicated to a single ingredient, see Jaine, p. 62. 'decapitation': Mennell, p. 206. On the lack of native models, see Grigson, p. xiii. On Escoffier and mint sauce, see Revel,

p. 223. On scurvy and constipation in English schools, see Drummond and Wilbraham, p. 340. 'Take Beetroot . . .': quoted in Brears, *et al.*, p. 293. For the English writer on salads of our own day, see Anderson, pp. 17–20. For meat in the England of Muskett's day, see Freeman, pp. 53–55. For their cousins in New South Wales, see Walker and Roberts, pp. 1 l, 20. On tea and its significance in nineteenth-century England, see Mintz, esp. pp. 110, 118–122, 138–150.

### t is for table talk

What little I know about the *Daijosai* comes from Sayle. 'one can consecrate himself . . .': Kakuzo, pp. 43, 52–53. The meals shared by women in the United Arab Emirate are described in Kanafani, pp. 15–17. 'If dolts think that it is a great . . .': Jacques Tahureau, *Les Dialogues* (1565), quoted in Jeanneret, p. 93. The rule of silence in monastic life is laid down in the Rule of St Benedict, xxxviii (translated in Bettenson, p. 121). The exclusive nature of the Greek *symposion* and Aristophanes' view of it is discussed in Oswyn Murray, 'The Affair of the Mysteries: Democracy and the Drinking Group', in Murray (ed.), pp. 149–161 (much that I have said about the *symposion* is deeply indebted to the essays in Murray's collection). For the nature of conversation in Plato's *Symposion*, see Kenneth Dover, introduction to Plato, p. 11. 'This is what you should say by the fire . . .': Xenophanes, quoted in Wolfgang Rösler, '*Mnemosyne* in the *Symposion*', in Murray (ed.), pp. 230–237, especially p. 232. Plutarch's observations are quoted by Jeanneret, p. 36. My views of social life in the eighteenth-century city have been much influenced by Sennett, ch. iii. 'I wish to God that you wouldn't keep rubbing . . .': Russell, p. 80. 'extremely free upon wholly undecent subjects . . .': quoted in Stone, p. 325 (see also Palmer, p. 23). The story of Byron's greed-disguised-as-sexism is related in Gronow, p. 121.

### U is for undead

Barber provides a remarkably intelligent and thorough account of vampiric folklore. He deals with garlic and other apotropaics on pp. 47–49. 'To those persons who may think . . .': quoted in a passage from Dr W.T. Fernie's *Health to Date* (1911), in Davidson, pp. 185–186: Davidson also includes (pp. 156–157) an article by Birgit Siesby on the use of blood in various cultures. On the protective use of garlic, see Senn, pp. 59–60. For the *aswang*, see Dresser, p. 75. McGee (1986) has a brief account (p. 156) of the mechanism by which the smell of garlic is released. Senn has a single reference (p. 119) to the use of garlic as a means of vampire detection. 'The smell of this plant . . .': Isabella Beeton, *Household Management* (1861), quoted in Gowers, p. 280 (who also quotes from Evelyn's *Acetaria* of 1699). Gowers, pp. 280–296, is my source for Roman views on garlic. The case I have presented against the Dolphin hypothesis is drawn from Dresser, pp. 177–199, and Barber, pp. 99– 100. Barber discusses attitudes to the recently dead on pp. 99, 196–197, and Senn mentions Romanian beliefs on p. 40.

### V is for venery
For Casanova on aphrodisiacs, see Wheaton, p. 159. 'representations of the *membra virilia* . . .': Richard Warner, *Antiquitates culinariae* (1791), quoted in Mintz, p. 243. For the French ambassador in Venice, see Wheaton, pp. 157–158. For Kettner's, see David, p. 195, and for Hugo's little black book see Wechberg, pp. 145–146.

### W is for weather
For Indian food in India and in England, see Burton, pp. 7–9, 75; for Indian food at the Cecil Hotel, see David (1984), p. 97. 'You must flay a Muscovite alive . . .': Montesquieu, vol. I, p. 223 (I have also used the translations of Montesquieu in Richter, especially pp. 257–260). 'Food becomes blood . . .': quoted in Kamenka, p. 111. The Thai expression is quoted, p. 6, by Thompson, who goes on to observe, quite correctly, that the Thai phrase is more encompassing than the axiom, 'You are what you eat'. Unfortunately, he attributes the latter to Brillat-Savarin.

### X is for Xanadu
'poverty and oysters always seem to go together . . .': quoted in Drummond and Wilbraham, p. 309.

## y is for yam

See Salaman, pp. 234–235, for an account of how the potato survived the English onslaught. The references to the role of *fan* in Chinese society are from Vera Y.N. Hsu and Francis L.K. Hsu, 'Modern China: North', in Chang (ed.), pp. 300–303, and from p. 14 of Chang's introduction. 'Porridge is food . . .': quoted in Murcott, p. 123. For the Bemba, see Mintz, pp. 9–12.

## Z is for zakuski

On the Victorian practice of eating jam before meat, see Drummond and Wilbraham, p. 281. For the smörgåsbord, see Luard, pp. 54–57.

# bibliography

[Abbot, Edward]: *The English and Australian Cookery Book* (1864) repr. as *The Colonial Cook Book* (Sydney, 1970).

Acton, Eliza: *Modern Cookery for Private Families* (1845; new ed., Lewes, East Sussex, 1993).

Adams, Douglas: *The Restaurant at the End of the Universe* (London, 1980).

Alexander, Stephanie: *Stephanie's Seasons* (Sydney, 1993).

Amis, Martin: *The Rachel Papers* (London, 1973).

Ancelet, Barry Jean; Edwards, Jay D. and Pitre, Glen: *Cajun Country* (Jackson and London, 1991).

Anderson, Digby: *The Spectator Book of Imperative Cooking* (London, 1987).

Anon: *The Boke of Kervynge* (London, 1508; facs. repr., Amsterdam and New York, 1971).

Aristophanes: *The Wasps*, trans. David Barrett (Harmondsworth, 1964).

Bachelard, Gaston: *The Psychoanalysis of Fire* [*La Psychoanalyse du Feu*, 1938], translated by Alan C. M. Ross (London, 1987).

Bailey, Stephen: *Taste: The Secret Meaning of Things* (London, 1991).

Barber, Paul: *Vampires, Burial, and Death* (New Haven and London, 1988).

Barley, Nigel: *The Innocent Anthropologist* (1983; new ed., Harmondsworth, 1986).

Barr, Ann and Levy, Paul: *The Official Foodie Handbook* (Australian ed., Sydney, 1985).

Barthes, Roland: *Mythologies* [*Mythologies*, 1957], translated by Annette Lavers (London, 1973).

Barthes, Roland: *Roland Barthes by Roland Barthes* [*Roland Barthes par Roland Barthes*, 1975], translated by Richard Howard (London, 1977).

Barthes, Roland: *Empire of Signs* [*L'Empire des Signes*, 1970], translated by Richard Howard (New York 1982).

Bateman, Michael: 'Simply Alastair', *The Independent on Sunday*, 19 September, 1993, review section, p. 45.

Beer, Maggie: *Maggie's Farm* (Sydney, 1993).

Bettenson, Henry (ed.): *Documents of the Christian Church* (2nd ed., Oxford, 1963).

Borges, Jorge Luis: 'The Argentine Writer and Tradition', in Borges, *Labyrinths: Selected Stories and Other Writings*, edited and translated by Donald A. Yates and James E. Irby (Harmondsworth, 1970).

Boswell, James: *The Life of Samuel Johnson* (1791; ed. Rodney Hall Shewan, 2 vols., London, 1968).

Bradbury, Malcolm: *Cuts* (London, 1987).

Brears, Peter; Black, Maggie; Corbishley, Gill; Renfrew, Jane and Stead, Jennifer: *A Taste of History: 10,000 Years of Food in Britain* (London, 1993).

Brillat-Savarin, Jean Anthelme: *The Physiology of Taste* [*La Physiologie du goût*, 1825], translated and annotated by M. F. K. Fisher (San Francisco, 1986).

Burton, David: *The Raj at Table* (London, 1993).

Burton, Nathaniel and Lombard, Rudy: *Creole Feast* (New York, 1978).

Carlier, Alexandra: *Ten Late Breakfasts* (London, 1988).

Castelvetro, Giacomo: *The Fruit, Herbs and Vegetables of Italy* [*Brieve racconte di tutte la radici, di tutte l'erbe e di tutti i frutti, che crudi o cotti in Italia si mangiano*, 1614], translated by Gillian Riley (London, 1989).

Chang, K. C. (ed.): *Food in Chinese Culture* (New Haven and London, 1977).

Collins, Rima and Richard: *The New Orleans Cookbook* (New York, 1989).

Comfort, Alex: *The Joy of Sex* (London, 1973).

Conrad, Glenn R. (ed.): *The Cajuns: Essays on Their History and Culture* (Lafayette, 1983).

Corones, Anthony; Pont, Graham and Santich, Barbara (eds.), *Food in Festivity: Proceedings of the Fourth Symposium of Australian Gastronomy* (Sydney, 1990).

Cowan, Ruth Schwartz: *More Work for Mother* (London, 1989).

Dale, David: *An Australian in America* (Sydney, 1988).

David, Elizabeth: *A Book of Mediterranean Food* (1950; new ed., London, 1988).

David, Elizabeth: *An Omelette and a Glass of Wine* (London, 1984).

Davidson, Alan (ed.): *On Fasting and Feasting* (London, 1988).

Davies, R.T. (ed.): *Medieval English Lyrics* (London, 1963).

Daws, Gavin: *Shoal of Time: A History of the Hawaiian Islands* (Honolulu, 1968).

Detienne, Marcel and Vernant, Jean-Pierre: *The Cuisine of Sacrifice among the Greeks* [*La cuisine du sacrifice en pays grecs*, 1979], translated by Paula Wissing (Chicago and London, 1989).

Douglas, Mary: *Purity and Danger: an Analysis of the Concepts of Pollution and Taboo* (London, 1966).

Dresser, Norine: *American Vampires: Fans, Victims and Practitioners* (New York and London, 1989).

Driver, Christopher: *The British at Table, 1940–1980* (London, 1983).

Dronke, Peter: *The Medieval Lyric* (2nd ed., London, 1978).

Drummond, J. C. and Wilbraham, Anne: *The Englishman's Food* (new ed., London, 1957).

Eisenstein, Elizabeth L: *The Printing Press as an Agent of Change* (Cambridge, 1979).

Elias, Norbert: *The Civilising Process: The Development of Manners* [*Uber den Prozess der Zivilisation*, 1939], translated by Edmund Jephcott (New York, 1968).

Esquivel, Laura: *Like Water for Chocolate*, translated by Carol Christensen and Thomas Christensen (new ed., London, 1993).

Fisher, M. F. K: *Serve it Forth* (1937) and *An Alphabet for Gourmets* (1949), repr. in *The Art of Eating* (new ed., New York, 1990).

Freeman, Sarah: *Mutton and Oysters: the Victorians and their Food* (London, 1989).

Giacosa, Ilaria Gozzini: *A Taste of Ancient Rome* [*A cena da Lucullo*, 1986], translated by Anna Herlotz (Chicago and London, 1992).

Goldhill, Simon: *Aeschylus: The Oresteia* (Cambridge, 1992).

Goncourt, Edmond and Jules de: *Pages from the Goncourt Journal*, edited, translated and introduced by Robert Baldick (Oxford, 1978).

Gowers, Emily: *The Loaded Table: Representations of Food in Roman Literature* (Oxford, 1993).

Gray, Patience: *Honey from a Weed* (London, 1986).

Grigson, Jane: *English Food* (rev. ed., Harmondsworth, 1993).

Gronow, Rees Howell: *The Reminiscences and Recollections of Captain Gronow* (1862–66), ed., John Raymond (London, 1964).

Guinaudeau, Z: *Fez: Traditional Moroccan Cooking*, translated from the French by J. E. Harris (Saint-Cloud, 1976).

Guste, Roy F., Jr: *Antoine's Restaurant, since 1840, Cookbook* (New York and London, 1980).

Gutierrez, C. Paige: *Cajun Foodways* (Jackson and London, 1992).

Harris, Marvin: *Good to Eat: the Riddles of Food and Culture* (London, 1988).

Hotteterre le Romain, Jacques: *Principles of the Flute, Recorder and Oboe* [*Principes de la Flûte Traversiére, . . . de la Flûte à bec, . . . et du Haut-Bois*, 1707], translated by David Lasocki (London, 1968).

Isaacs, Jennifer: *Bush Food* (Sydney, 1987).

Jaine, Tom (ed.): *Oxford Symposium on Food and Cookery 1987* (London, 1988).

Jaine, Tom: 'Banquets and Meals', in Barbara Santich and Michael Symons (eds.), *Proceedings of the Fifth Symposium of Australian Gastronomy* (Adelaide, 1991), pp. 61–63.

James, Clive: *Unreliable Memoirs* (London, 1980).

Jeanneret, Michel: *A Feast of Words: Banquets and Table Talk in the Renaissance* [*Des mets et des mots*, 1987], translated by Jeremy Whiteley and Emma Hughes (London, 1991).

Kakuzo, Okakura: *The Book of Tea: A Japanese Harmony of Art, Culture and the Simple Life* (Sydney, 1932).

Kalčik, Susan: 'Ethnic Foodways in America: Symbol and the

Performance of Identity', in Linda Keller Brown and Kay Mussell (eds.), *Ethnic and Regional Foodways in the United States* (Knoxville, 1984), pp. 37–65.

Kamenka, Eugene: *The Philosophy of Ludwig Feuerbach* (London, 1970).

Kanafani, Aida S: *Aesthetics and Ritual in the United Arab Emirates: The Anthropology of Food and Personal Adornments among Arabian Women* (Beirut, 1983).

Keates, Jonathan: *Handel: The Man and his Music* (London, 1985).

Kodama-Nishomoto, Michi; Nishimoto, Warren S; and Oshiro, Cynthia A, (eds.): *Hanahana: An Oral History Anthology of Hawaii's Working People* (Honolulu, 1984).

Kuykendall, Ralph S: *The Hawaiian Kingdom 1778–1854: Foundation and Transformation* (Honolulu, 1938).

Lévi-Strauss, Claude: *The Raw and the Cooked* [*Le Cru et le cuit*, 1964] translated by John and Doreen Weightman (Harmondsworth, 1986).

Levy, Paul: *Out to Lunch* (London, 1986).

Luard, Elisabeth: *European Peasant Cookery* (London, 1986).

MacClancy, Jeremy: *Consuming Culture* (London, 1992).

MacDonogh, Giles: *A Palate in Revolution: Grimod de La Reynière and the 'Almanach des Gourmands'* (London, 1987).

McCullough, Colleen: *The First Man in Rome* (London, 1990).

McGee, Harold: *On Food and Cooking: the Science and Lore of the Kitchen* (London, 1986).

McGee, Harold: *The Curious Cook* (London, 1992).

Mennell, Stephen: *All Manners of Food: Eating and Taste in England and France from the Middle Ages to the Present* (Oxford, 1985).

Minor, Andrew C. and Mitchell, Bonner: *A Renaissance Entertainment* (Columbia, Missouri, 1968).

Mintz, Sidney W: *Sweetness and Power: The Place of Sugar in Modern History* (New York, 1985).

Mollison, Bill: *The Permaculture Book of Ferment and Human Nutrition* (Tyalgum, NSW, 1993).

Montesquieu, Charles Louis de Secondat, Baron de: *The Spirit of the Laws* [*De l'Esprit des Lois*, 1748], translated by Thomas Nugent (repr. New York and London, 1949, two volumes in one).

Murcott, Anne: 'You Are What You Eat: Anthropological Factors

Influencing Food Choice', in C. Ritson, L. Golton and J. McKenzie (eds.), *The Food Consumer* (London, 1986) pp.107–125.

Murray, Oswyn (ed.): *Sympotica: A Symposium on the 'Symposion'* (Oxford, 1990).

Muskett, Philip E: *The Art of Living in Australia* (Sydney, 1893; facs. repr., Sydney, 1987).

Oakeshott, Michael: *Rationalism in Politics and Other Essays* (London, 1962).

Obeyesekere, Gananath: *The Apotheosis of Captain Cook: European Mythmaking in the Pacific* (Princeton, 1992).

Page, Christopher: 'The Performance of Songs in Late Medieval France', *Early Music* vol. 10, 1982, pp. 441–450.

Page, Christopher: *Voices and Instruments of the Middle Ages* (London, 1987).

Palmer, Arnold: *Moveable Feasts: a Reconnaissance of the Origins and Consequences of Fluctuations in Meal-Times with Special Attention to the Introduction of Luncheon and Afternoon Tea* (1952; new ed., Oxford, 1984).

*Picayune's Creole Cook Book* (2nd ed., New Orleans, 1901; repr., New York, 1971).

Plato: *Symposium*, ed., Kenneth Dover (Cambridge, 1980).

Porter, Roy: *English Society in the Eighteenth Century* (Harmondsworth, 1982).

Pyne, Stephen: *Burning Bush: a Fire History of Australia* (Sydney, 1992).

Rees, Nigel: *Slogans* (London, 1982).

Revel, Jean-François: *Culture and Cuisine* [*Un festin en paroles*, 1979], translated by Helen R. Lane (New York, 1982).

Richie, Donald: *A Taste of Japan* (Tokyo and New York, 1985).

Richter, Melvin: *The Political Theory of Montesquieu* (Cambridge, 1977).

Riley, Gillian: *Renaissance Recipes* (San Francisco, 1993).

Roden, Claudia: *A New Book of Middle Eastern Food* (Harmondsworth, 1986).

Roden, Claudia: *The Food of Italy* (London, 1989).

Rossotti, Hazel: *Fire* (Oxford, 1993).

Russell, George W. E.: *Collections and Recollections* (London, 1903).

Sahlins, Marshall: *Culture and Practical Reason* (Chicago and London, 1976).

Sahlins, Marshall: *Historical Metaphors and Mythical Realities: Structure in the Early History of the Sandwich Islands Kingdom* (Ann Arbor, 1981).

Sahlins, Marshall: *Anahulu, the Anthropology of History in the Kingdom of Hawaii: Historical Ethnography* (Chicago, 1992).

Salaman, Redcliffe: *The History and Social Influence of the Potato* (1949; new ed., Cambridge, 1985).

Salter, H. E. (ed.): *Registrum Annalium Collegii Mertonensis, 1483–1521 (Oxford Historical Society (Series)*, LXXVI, Oxford, 1923).

Santich, Barbara and Symons, Michael (eds.): *Proceedings of the Third Symposium of Australian Gastronomy* (Adelaide, 1988).

Satterwhite, Robb: *What's What in Japanese Restaurants* (Tokyo and New York, 1988).

Sayle, Murray: 'The Emperor and the Sun Goddess', *The Spectator*, 12 November 1990, pp. 10–12.

Schama, Simon: *The Embarrassment of Riches: An Interpretation of Dutch Culture in the Golden Age* (London, 1987).

Senn, Harry A.: *Were-Wolf and Vampire in Romania* (Boulder and New York, 1982).

Sennett, Richard: *The Fall of Public Man* (New York, 1977).

Shintani, Terry, and Hughes, Claire, (eds.): *The Wai'anae Book of Hawaiian Health* (Wai'anae, 1992).

Stone, Lawrence: *The Family, Sex and Marriage in England 1500–1800* (rev. ed., Harmondsworth, 1979).

[Swift, Jonathan]: *A Complete Collection of Genteel and Ingenious Conversation . . . by Simon Wagstaff, Esq.* (1738), ed. [as *Swift's Polite Conversation*] Eric Partridge (London, 1963).

Tate, Merze: *Hawaii: Reciprocity or Annexation* (East Lansing, 1968).

Thompson, David: *Classic Thai Cuisine* (Sydney, 1993).

Trilling, Diana: *The Beginning of the Journey* (San Diego, 1994).

Walker, Robin and Roberts, David: *From Scarcity to Surfeit: A History of Food and Nutrition in New South Wales* (Sydney, 1988).

Weinstock, Herbert: *Rossini: a Biography* (London, 1968).

Wechberg, Joseph: *Blue Trout and Black Truffles: the Peregrinations of an Epicure* (London, 1953).

Wheaton, Barbara Ketcham: *Savouring the Past: The French Kitchen and Table from 1300 to 1789* (London, 1983).

Willan, Anne: *Great Cooks and their Recipes from Taillevent to Escoffier* (London, 1992).

Xenophon: *The Drinking Party* [*Symposion*], in *Conversations of Socrates*, translated by Hugh Tredennick and Robyn Waterfield (Harmondsworth, 1990).